A SEAHOUSES SAG

by

Andrew Craig Rutte

GW00385245

First published 1998.

ISBN   0 9526496 1 6

British Library Cataloguing-in-Publication Data. A catalogue record for this book is available from the British Library.

Published by F.L.Kennington, Northumbria House, 35, Corbar Road, Stockport, Cheshire.   SK2 6EP.

Printed by Parchment(Oxford) Ltd., Printworks, Crescent Road, Cowley, Oxford.   OX4 2PB.

Acknowledgments :-
'to all those good folks who gave me impetus and encouragement to write this book - my sincere thanks'.
'to Katrina Porteous, author in her own right, for her generous and unstinting help in getting this launched.'
'to Brian and Doreen Short for the loan of old photographs.'
'to Geoffrey Stewart for his contribution of photographs.'
'to my family who patiently deciphered and typed my script.'

1

CONTENTS.

1.   In the beginning   Page   5

2.   Early fishing days.   17

3.   The Spoken Word.   30

4.   Of visitors and boats.   37

5.   The Harbour.   56

6.   Stranger than fiction.........   63

7.   Grace Darling.   67

8.   In lighter vein.   72

9.   The Northumbrian coble.   75

10.   'The Wulker'.   95

Cover: Seahouses Harbour c.1910.

Rear cover (inset):   The Author at home, May 1998.

ILLUSTRATIONS.

Page.

10 Seahouses fishermen on a Sunday morning in the 1920s.

22 The 'Speedwell', the last keelboat working out of Seahouses.

36 The Rutter family keelboat.

47 Local boats in Seahouses - 1905/1910.

48 Local and Scottish boats c.1910.

50 Seahouses Harbour c.1908, all sail boats.

52 Harbour from the Magazine c.1905.

55 The Outer Harbour at low tide. 1910.

60 Cornish Luggers from St.Ives c.1905.

63 A 1930s view with Scottish boats.

65 The 'Supreme' from Fisherrow, 1930s.

68 The freighter 'Hanna Holken' in harbour.

73 The Author's Uncle, John Allen.

76 The 'Emperor', a 3 planked sailing coble.

79 The 'Boy's Pride', a 4 planked sailing coble.

82 The 'Clan Gillean', a 5 planked motor coble.

86 The Northumbrian Sailing Coble No.1
87   do   No.2.
88   do   No.3

94 Every newly-married man's work A fishing stool.

INTRODUCTION.

This is the story of a Northumberland fishing village, of its people, and the boats they sailed in. About a fishing community through the eyes of one of the fishermen who was born into that community in 1912.

It is in memory of all those who made their living from the sea.

'Why don't you write it all down before its lost?' they said. 'Not enough education', I replied.
'Not to worry', they said, 'just go ahead, the same as if you were talking to us'.

So, if you are expecting a learned treatise, full of high flown phrases and long nebbit words, or even grammatically correct, then I'm sorry, it may fall a bit short. I've tried to do what they said and done it as if I were talking. But conversations may high-light other views or even disagreements.

Be that as it may, having never written a book before, here I go, one step at a time, like crossing Waren Slakes in a fog!.

Read on then, if you so desire, but do not say you did not get fair warning!.

Andrew Rutter,
Seahouses, 1997.

Where the name 'SUNDERLAND' is used, it refers, of course, to 'NORTH SUNDERLAND, Northumberland'.

'Fathers and Sons' entering Seahouses Harbour in a northerly blow.

An oil painting by the Author

IN THE BEGINNING........

Seahouses has a long history. I have to start somewhere so where better that to relate a bit of history so that things fall into place. If you aren't 'into history', don't despair, the bits about boats, fish, scuba divers come later. You could skip a page, I don't mind!.

North Sunderland Seahouses, to give it its full title, is an area inhabited since the Iron Age at least. There are numerous remains of burial sites, but not of dwellings, except on Budle Crags, just west of the caravan site.

The most important site was discovered during excavations for the water reservoir at the top of the rise west of Seafield Farm, now surrounded by caravans. It had been a cemetery with stone cists, the skeletons in a sitting position facing the rising sun, with pottery urns beside them. On exposure to the air the bones crumbled to dust. Some were six feet tall – big men! My Uncle Harry Allen told me this, having witnessed the opening of some of the tombs. I do not know what happened to the pottery – but, so far as I know none of the caravanners have been haunted – so the Ancient Brits must have been a quiet lot!

On 30th May 1862, when digging a drain at the Blue Bell Inn, North Sunderland, a stone cist of the usual form was discovered, a foot below the surface, although in earlier digging, more than three feet of earth had been removed. The cist consisted of six flagstones, four side stones, a corner stone and a stone bottom. It was 38 inches long; 21 inches wide; and 20 inches deep.

It contained the remains of a girl about nine years old, laid on her side, with head towards the rising sun, also three pottery vessels.

Shortly after the end of the last war, a tomb was discovered just south of Monkshouse, when sand was blown away revealing grave marking stones above the surface. This one was not a cist in the true sense, merely smallish flat stones between 12 and 18 inches wide set edge up around the remains of the skeleton of a young woman. It had no covering stone.

Possibly more remains are buried in the dunes, as drowned sailors in the old days were usually buried where they were washed ashore. There used to be two similarly made graves in the peat on the Outer Wideopens. When my father was a young man, he saw the outline of a man's skeleton in the peat on the top of the South Wamses, but he could never find it again.

From the Iron Age to the coming of the Romans is a big leap, but has the advantage of lifting the lid a little.

The Romans tramped pretty much all over the British Isles, spending some time in what they called Caledonia, later to become Scotland. Either the climate or the terrain did not suit, or the natives proved uncooperative, as the Romans, having stayed in the Lowlands behind the earth wall from the Forth to the Clyde, consolidated their hold on Britain by building Hadrians Wall from the North Sea to the Solway thus leaving the Northern tribes to themselves.

It has been established that a Roman outpost existed on the rocky knowes west of Waren Mill and probably they had a foothold on the crag now occupied by Bamburgh Castle. Little has come to light of their stay, hidden for ever in the mists of time.

More or less co-inciding with the collapse of the Roman Empire and the gradual withdrawal of the Legions came the influx of the first settlers from the Continent, the Anglo-Saxons. Despite opposition by the native Roman-Brits they soon established a strong hold in the eastern sea-board lands. These people were the corn growers crossing the narrow seas in their clinker built iron-clenched ships, not as well designed or as shapely as the later Norse vessels, for example, the Nydam ship or the Sutton Hoo.

The next three centuries saw the formation of petty kingdoms, the former occupants being edged south and west, until the country was mostly in Anglo-Saxon hands. In turn, they themselves came under pressure from Scandinavian tribes from Denmark, Norway, Sweden and the South Baltic coasts, also on the hunt for land.

One of the most powerful, if not the most powerful of the Anglo-Saxon kingdoms was Northumbria – the land north of the Humber. It stretched from the Humber to the Firth of Forth and well into the western hinterland where it kept up sporadic warfare with the Celtic speaking tribes. Northumbria was itself divided into two parts, the south from the Humber to the Tyne, and the north from the Tyne to the Firth of Forth. This northern half was called Bernicia or Beornicia, the southern half, Deira.

Celtic mystics in the west were founding Christian establishments and branching out to bring the new religion to the Angles, Saxons and Scandinavian settlers. A missionary from Iona, Aidan, was the first according to the history books. He was followed by Paulinus who had a field day baptising the locals at Gefrin, near Wooler.

It is nowise my intention to write the history of Northumberland, but merely to try to show that the Seahouses area was inhabited.

The 'Bede' history is about the only source of information about these dark ages and even that is subject to conjecture.

So we come to the year 685 when Ecgfrith was King and ruled from the Tyne to the Forth but wanted to extend his influence at the expense of other people. He took his army of merry men and an army of Danes across the Forth into Fife and thereabouts to wallop Brude, King of the Picts, whose land it was. He bit off more than he could chew and was just about wiped off the map at a place called Nechtansmere or Dunnichen Moss in Angus. Tradition has it that a lone survivor made it back across the Firth some time later.

The outcome was that Northumberland was at the mercy of any warlord who fancied it. Meantime, in Europe, Christianity was working slowly northwards and in 782, Charlemagne, the christian King of France, in a flurry of religious zeal, took the faith at the point of the sword and beat the heathen Saxons at Verdun.

He offered his 4500 prisoners the choice of accepting the new faith or death. They clung to their warlike Nordic gods with great tenacity, so they were put to the sword.

News of the massacre filtered through the Nordic world, hatred of Christianity was fuelled, starting the Viking raids in revenge, including that on Lindisfarne in 793.

Prayers were said, asking God to deliver them from the 'fury of the Northmen' who got the reputation of being 'ravening wolves' but in truth were no worse than the rest of mankind. To Nordic standards the slaughter of helpless prisoners was a shameful act. Remember also that the Nordic people gave us our conception of democratic government. They practised a primitive form of fair play; their ideal death was a brave one on the battlefields, looking on death in bed from old age or whatever as a 'cow's death'.

Britain, especially the east side in the early years, had strong Norse connections. The Scandinavian kingdoms of Norway, Sweden and Denmark sent forth exploration parties, founding settlements in the Faroes, Iceland, Greenland (so named to attract would-be settlers, but possibly less harsh in climate then) and eventually reaching the coast of America. There they attempted to settle but failed, owing as much as anything to the distance from the parent country.

By a very early date the Angles had settled around our local area, establishing 'townships' as the various farm settlements were called, all within a reasonable distance from the central stronghold on the great crag of Bamburgh. 'Bebbansburgh' was named, it is said, after an Angle chieftainess of whom little is known except her name and the date of 607.

That the area had a strong influx of Norse speakers in later years was due to the fact that Eric Bloodaxe, a Norwegian king who had been deposed, was making himself a nuisance on the Northumbrian coast, so the English King Athelstan made him the governor, with headquarters at Bamburgh, to keep him quiet. He would doubtless find employment for his merry men also, and so in the year 937 we had our local Norsemen.

Eric got his final come-uppance somewhere in Durham in Edred's reign and is buried thereabouts.

In 993 a pair of 'Danes' named Justin and Guthmund captured Bamburgh Castle but history is vague and leaves much unsaid.

So, all in all, it had been a pretty hectic locality to live in then.

As folk had to eat to live, ordinary people must have carried on with their small crofts, raising a few cereals and keeping a few sheep and cattle, driving them into thickets when danger loomed.

The coastal settlements were at least a short half mile from the sea to allow time to flee in case of a seaboard landing. Seahouses Beadnell, Newton and Howick were all cases in point. I almost forgot to include the lost village of Shoreston which appeared in the later Norman Rolls under various spellings. Funny how ancient memories persisted when I was a small boy. I remember my mother telling me that fishermen used to live at Shorestone, as it was spelt 75 years ago and that they kept their boats at Monkshouse Haven (of which more anon).

The pundits will tell you that in this area at least, most of the place names are Anglo-Saxon and that Norse influence was so minimal as to be ignored entirely! So what? Anglo-Saxon was no doubt understood by the Norse speakers. The Angles had named their holdings many years before and it would be therefore a hard thing not to refer to them by their established names, even by the Norsemen. While the Northumbrian speech, especially in the northern and western area, if written down, comes up as Lowland Scots. You have to hear it spoken by a native to realise that with all its subtle inflexions and complexities, it contains a strong Norse underlay even to modern times. Several times among the Gaelic speakers of the Western Isles I have been taken for a Shetlander and some of our local words are the same as used in Shetland speech. But I digress, so I'll get back to the mainstream again.

After mostly unco-ordinated resistance by the locals, the Normans, once they were firmly rooted, proceeded to rampage through the land, grabbing the best bits, building castles and strongholds, generally terrorising the locals into submission, and forcing them to labour to supply them with food for a start. To give them their due, the Normans were good at keeping records of their businesses and so we come at last to a period when some sort of historical records were established. There were language difficulties for a long time but gradually the French speech died away and recognisable English was beginning to emerge. As all the King's favourites got the plum estates, quite a lot of Normans thought they should have done better. As Scottish Nationalism was beginning to boil, they took the opportunity to jump aboard the Scottish band waggon, switching allegiances with great aplomb. So there was to-ing and fro-ing, wheeling, dealing and skulduggery by the bucketful. Murder and mayhem were committed to achieve their ends.

The Normans were not long in grabbing Bamburgh, that strong ancient fortress, the royal Bernician seat. How the locals viewed their new bosses we do not know, but what is recorded is that they had to render service to the new owners by work in the fields and to supply firewood for the castle fires. Coal was also dug in the bell-shaped shafts on Belford Moor and carried on mule or horseback.

A demarcation line was roughly established, sometimes south of the Tweed, sometimes north, and eventually on it on its lower reaches. Unfortunately this cut Bernicia in half together with its inhabitants who were brain-washed to the extent that, south of the Tweed they were 'English', and north as far as the Firth of Forth they were 'Scots'. Thus a people were divided and set against one another by powers beyond their control and for centuries thereafter were forced to girn at each other as 'enemies'. It was a natural nursery for all the subsequent troubles that plagued its inhabitants thereafter.

The outcome of all this was that, while the southern part of England was achieving a measure of stability, Northumberland was the main battleground for the English and Scots when they came to blows. How the unfortunate inhabitants managed to survive at all speaks well for their tenacity and ability to endure.

9

Seahouses fishermen on a Sunday morning in the 1920s, including some of the Author's relatives. L to R: Jim Robson; Michael Robson (Cloggie); Uncle Bob Rutter; Ralph Spiers; Father; John Rutter; Uncle Henry Allen; Jack Sheil; George Dawson (the Gull); Will Swan; Billy Nelson (Toddy). Taken by Harry Nelson.

In Edward II's reign in 1318, a complaint was sent to the King that Roger de Horsley, the governor of Bamburgh Castle, was charging the men of Sunderland and Shorston exorbitant rents for the poor shelters they had to provide themselves within the Castle walls in time of trouble 'so that those who were supposed to be our protectors were worse than the Scots'. The King directed they should not be charged.

About 100 years before the Normans, Malcolm of Scotland had Cumbria under his sway, and later, from 1139 to 1157, Northumberland was also Scottish with the exception of the Castles of Newcastle and Bamburgh. How they worked that little lot out is not recorded, but for a time it must have been an amicable arrangement.

Now the Normans, with their passion for snooping into everybodys business, in case they were being done out of a groat or two, got all those who could wield a pen, mostly from the monkish orders, to make a record of everybody in the country and what they possessed by way of goods and chattels – a medieval Who's Who.

Coming back to this area, the local peasants were forced to till certain fields, cart hay and grain, firewood and other goods to the castle at Bamburgh.

In the early 1300s the men of Sunderland and Shorston were employed as carriers both by land and water. Their journeys between the Tweed and Coquet rivers were varied by taking goods by boat from Sunderland to the Castle garrison. These sea–borne goods were mainly provisions. So, here we have the first reference to the locally owned boats which must have been big enough and sturdy enough to carry cargo. Years earlier, the monks of Lindisfarne used boats for fishing and for visiting the nearby Fahran Islands (note the old spelling)

What manner of boats these were we have no way of knowing but I'd guess they were a simple model of wooden construction, clench built in the Norse manner. I think there is a reference somewhere to the Abbot of Lindisfarne ordering two new boats.

I cannot see the seamen of this time using skin–covered coracles as some historians assert. They were the Celts idea of boats, and while they were certainly in use on the west side, they would be an object of derision to the people of Northern descent on this side.

We know there were Irish monks among the first missionaries here

but they were visiting and preaching to people, who, if not themselves their forebears, had crossed the North Sea in wooden boats of
no mean size. They had had experience in marine architecture,
some of their models showing great sophistication and forethought,
with sound sea-keeping principles firmly established.

Granted the Celts did remarkable voyages in them, but like their
modern counterparts – the Curraghs of Ireland and Coracles of
Wales – their ability to ride the sea was due more to the skill of
their handlers than to innovative design in hull form.

I have neglected to mention that we had two Norse infiltrations, one
from the east, one from the south west via Cumbria and Lancashire.
When the Irish finally got the upper hand and drove the Norsemen
out, they settled in the Isle of Man, then Cumbria, then Yorkshires
Dales and through the Borders.

Their sense of independence was evident in their descendants for it
was not until the Union of the Crowns in 1603 that they were
persuaded finally to bow to authority.

Northumbria was 'terra incognito', and to be appointed to one of the
administrative posts was looked upon as a sign of Royal displeasure.
In other words, if you did'nt come up to scratch as a courtier then
you were banished to the Northern wilds.

Despite harsh reprisals the Border 'clans' on both sides were never
fully subdued. They were the despair of the various administrators
for the respective Crowns; edicts were passed forbidding contact or
marriage across the Border. These were promptly ignored as were
most other laws so they did as they liked, when they liked, and
generally cocked a snook at authority. Even when the Borders were
running at full blast there appear five names in the Muster Rolls for
Beadnell in 1538 appended as 'Scotsmen', living among their
supposed 'enemies'.

Land grabbing and Clearances happened here long before the
Highlanders suffered the same fate in the 19th Century, and for
much the same causes. Common land was stolen on piece. In the
latter part of Elizabeth 1 reign, Sir Thomas Gray of Chillingham
expelled 300 men, women and children from their homes at
Newham, not far inland, so that 'he could turn ye land to pasture'.
The old, now lost, village of Shorston could have suffered the same
fate. Whether by abandonment, eviction or plague it disappeared. I
imagine the site of the village was just west of Shoreston Hall,
between the west wall of the Hall grounds and Clashup Cottage,

where the road turns up to New Shoreston Farm. In the field, which is hummocked and has never been ploughed to my knowledge, there is an old spring house. It is the logical place for the village, standing high for good drainage, a small burn running past Clashup down to Monkshouse where it joins the Brock Burn from Fowberry and draining the low land west of the site.

And so, whatever happened, Shorston village was no more. The fishermen whose boats were kept at Monkshouse haven, not the one we know now, but one more protected from the elements by the high limestone reefs on either side before they were quarried off in later years. The deep ruts left by the carts that led the limestone away are still traceable in the underlying soft rock strata.

We come now to the time when the potential of making and exporting lime was realised. It had been made in small quantities throughout the ages. Opposite the Dunes Hotel was a considerable limestone outcrop on the shore, known locally as 'the Far Kilns'. While traces of burnt stone and ash are to be found in the cliff edge turf, no trace of the kilns remains. This would be very ancient lime burning purely for local use. There was a similar set up on the shore on entering Beadnell from the north, but with a man-made mound. This mound, opposite the Council camping area, was removed a few years ago.

It could be as much as 300 years ago when the great quarries were opened at Sunderland/Seahouses. A massive kiln was built on the shore, the top coming roughly level with the cliff top behind it. The gut that was formerly used by the local boatmen was deepened and enclosed with two stout and well built piers, large enough to hold the few small ships which used to transport the lime by sea. This is now the inner harbour, much modified in the 1880s, when the outer harbour was added to accomodate the huge increase in the herring fishing, of which more anon.

Now for centuries the local tenor of life would have been subsistence farming; some fishing, for local consumption, perhaps with some fish wind dried, salted, or otherwise cured. This was much like the way of life in the Northern Isles and the Hebrides until quite modern times.

What the village of Sunderland looked like we do not know as no traces of ancient buildings remain. We do know that a defensive tower existed on the site of St.Paul's Church at the top of the village but it was in ruins when it was removed in 1790 to make way for the Church.

I imagine the village would consist of 'buts and bens', single storey, earth floored cabins with thatched roofs and no drainage. They would be on both sides of a single street, as likely as not having a gate or 'yett' at each end to hold the livestock in case of invasion.

With the advent of the quarries a new element was introduced. Once the business was in operation, bringing fresh incomers, ships would arrive with red clay pantiles as ballast from Holland. Thus there would be a better class of cottage built with tiles rather than thatch; later they would be floored with flagstones from Caithness. Men would actually be getting paid for their labour, albeit not very much and a new era was dawning.

This was the first of the major changes to occur in the village. It was brought into contact with a wider world instead of being insulated from the mainstream of English influence and commerce. Foreign ships were coming and going, new ideas were being brought to bear, the old ways gone for ever. With the coming of the sailors a new trade developed – smuggling.

Revenue laws against spirits, fancy cloths and silk were avoided by men who established well run rackets, no doubt their way of thinking they were public benefactors!. The 'Newcastle Courant' of 26th February 1763 records that 'on 19th September 1762, a large quantity of goods belonging to Scottish smugglers was seized at Beadnell'. The haul included 2,700 gallons of brandy, 400 gallons of rum and 'geneva', 23 hogsheads of wine, some tea and other articles. Wailing and gnashing of teeth would doubtless follow!

Almost every local fisherman would be in on it. When all went well it was a fairly lucrative venture and a few more coins to swell the meagre returns from the fishing would be more than welcome.

In their view it was not a crime to defraud the customs – they were only going counterwise to the harsh import duties of the time.

Smuggling was rife all around the British Isles, and in a lot of cases, surprisingly well organised. Bloody, even fatal, clashes took place between the smugglers and the excisemen. It was regarded as romantic; pictures were painted depicting dashing smugglers landing their contraband in some wild seascape, complete with foreshore, cave, boats drawn up, horses and pack mules being loaded up, and brigandish figures draped around. That they had the blessing of the local gentry in many cases is undeniable, 'brandy for the parson, baccy for the clerk', sort of thing.

One of the notorious places hereabouts was Boulmer where began an 'underground' trail ending in the Border town of Jedburgh or 'Jeddart' as it was known in the old manner. Journeys were made during the hours of darkness, the pack train lying hidden in some remote farm steading or secluded glen during the day. If you sight a line from Boulmer to Jedburgh on an ordnance map it will pass fairly close to the village of Ellingham whose local pub is named the 'Pack Horse'. No doubt judicious quantities would be doled out on the journey to various places to oil the wheels so to speak!

Some of the young men from Seahouses went further afield, some went whaling for a season, some in merchant ships. One of my clan went voyaging to the Mediterranean and Naples, while my grandmother's uncle was in the H.M.S.Glorious when she was lost in Leith Roads early in the 1800s.

By the beginning of the 19th Century the white fishing i.e. ling, cod, haddock, whiting, etc., was done from the unique boats that are often erroneously called 'Yorkshire Cobles' which in point of fact should be the 'Northumbrian Coble' as they are general from Berwick to the Yorkshire coast. For the annual herring season a different type was used, being about 30 feet or more, double ended, very beamy and very strongly built in the Firth of Forth pattern, again of which more anon.

The quarries, to come back to them again, were owned in 1814 by the firm of Robson and Skelly. By the 1860s the owners had died out and they were in the sole ownership of a Miss Skelly. I think it was in 1865 that the last lot of lime was dried, ending the lime trade of North Sunderland.

In the meantime better houses had appeared, especially around the harbour area, some to house the kiln workers.

What is now the Old Ship Hotel was, I've heard, originally a farmhouse, and possibly the oldest building in the harbour area. A large high building was erected against the cliff at the head of the cove beach as a granary, there being another two in the village to store surplus locally grown corn. This was shipped out by sea until the advent of the main railway line between Newcastle and Edinburgh which passes only 5 miles to the west of the village.

Now this more or less coincided with the run down of the quarries and a lot of the quarrymen turned to fishing as better prices for fish were realised once it could be sent by train to the large towns. The initial journey to Chathill was by horse and cart. Prices for fish were surprisingly good for that day and age, comparing favourably with those we got here between the two World Wars.

By the 1860s and 70s local fishermen were following the herring shoals to Yarmouth and Lowestoft. The boats were the type now generally called 'Fifies', a much bigger version of those from the beginning of the century. They had two masts, were rigged with a dipping lug on the foremast and standing lug on the mizzen, also setting spare canvas in the shape of jibs and 3-cornered staysails. The bigger ones were 45/50 feet long with a cabin and coal stove in the fore part. Nets were hauled by a hand operated capstan called appropriately the 'Iron Man'.

Now this was the second major change. Herring was King. From the Shetlands to the English Channel they were pursued during the summer and autumn months by hundreds of boats, not only British but Dutch and French. Preserving the herring was by brine salt or by smoke drying salt herrings in wood smoke – these were the famous bloaters.

The continentals were great eaters of salt herring as were the ordinary people of this country and a lucrative trade developed in the export of salt herring in barrels as far afield as Russia. About the middle of the 19th century an English herring merchant named Woodger was at Seahouses for the herring season. He formulated a theory that by lightly salting a split open herring and smoke curing it overnight it would remain edible for at least a week even in the summer time. As the main line train was available they could be rushed to the centres of population from Newcastle to London in a few hours!.

It was said often enough by the village elders that his experiments took place in an outbuilding in what is now the yard of the Ship Hotel. I don't suppose success would be immediate as the proper method of making kippers is a highly skilled job and he was starting almost from scratch. After trial and error the secret was finally mastered and the first kipper made its debut on the fishmongers slab. It was a resounding success. The townies could not get enough of this new product. The herring yards which had been mostly concerned with salt herrings were hurriedly converted to handle the kippers. Old cottages adjacent to the yards were built up another storey – you can still see where the walls were made higher – and made into smoke houses. As the kippers were eaten largely in this country, it gave a tremendous fillip to the fishing industry which reached its peak just prior to the first World War.

That War finished the local herring fleet. The post-war landings were made by Scots boats. A brief upsurge was made after the second World War which, by using new methods, succeeded in reducing the shoals of herring almost to extinction.

We now examine the third and latest major change. What used to be a fishing village is now a village with few fishing boats and fishermen. Since the last war the village has grown to twice its former size and is peopled by incomers, mostly from further south, retired people and younger people commuting to Alnwick and Berwick. Some are employed in the village itself in various activities that have mushroomed into being. This had its beginning in the years after the first World War. It goes under the general title of 'Tourist Industry' when every summer we see the area thronged with holiday makers beguiled by the Northumbria Tourist Board brochures. The property around the focal point of the village – the harbour – has been evacuated almost entirely by the natives and the former fishermens' cottages converted to holiday homes.

So this is the background to the saga of North Sunderland and Sea-houses. The broad scope of the canvas has been painted, the next task is to fill in the details and make the picture a comprehensive whole.

2.   EARLY FISHING DAYS.

As a village expands, for whatever reason, it both loses and gains, but it is never ever the same in atmosphere again. It can reach the critical size where the original closeness of the inhabitants is destroyed, as has occurred here.

In the North Sunderland/Seahouses villages up until the second World War few changes had taken place since the turn of the century, forty years earlier. Before that time the main occupation was fishing which provided a living for about 80 men and also for numerous others ashore who provided the necessary bits and pieces They were the back up workers – coopers to make barrels; net makers, who also made the oilskins; cobblers who hand made the heavy leather thigh boots until the cheaper rubber ones took over; and not least the women who gutted, split, and salted the fish and followed their men to the seasonal fishing. If you were a boy born into this community there were few choices of occupation on leaving school. There were only three main ones:- fishing, farming or serving time in the building trade. The latter, even including house painting, was not extensive.

Fishermens' sons tended to follow their father's trade. Fishermens' daughters married fishermen for they had to have a wife to help, not only to keep house but to be part of their shore based work force.

In the fishing section of the community everybody had to 'turn to', especially during the winter months, when the main fishing for white fish was under way. Long lines averaging 1200 hooks per line had to be untangled, baited, and relaid each working day ready for the next day's fishing. The only relief came from the Sabbath break or weather bad enough to stop the boats getting to sea.

Going back to the 1880s, my parents young days, remembering what I was told as a child, and taking that time as a start for my tale, then up until the start of the first World War (1914) the life of the Northumbrian fishermen, in the northern part at least, was divided into seasons. From May until September the herring was pursued by the majority of the men. Only the old men kept on during the summer either hand lining for cod or working creaves, which are the traps for shellfish, crab and lobster. The cobles and mules were hauled ashore and the big herring boats overhauled painted and refurbished ready for the season. In September the big boats around 50 feet were got ready for the Yarmouth fishing, sail -ing with hundreds of Scottish boats down the eastern English coast, returning in November usually. Before laying up for the winter they went to Amble and loaded up with local coal to tide their home fires over until spring. Then the 'long line' for white fish started, lasting usually until early spring. Now in case of being misunderstood, I must explain at this point that these seasons were not rigidly regimented. The crews of the smaller herring boats which did not go to the English fishing at Yarmouth or Lowestoft would go for lobsters after September for some months before the long lining. If fish were scarce after New Year, creaves would be shot for crabs and lobsters until the start of the new herring season. Thus there were three main sources of making a living and fishermen tended to go to the one they imagined would pay best at the time.

As this way of life has vanished I'll do my best to record it as it was.

The herring fishing year usually started in the Northern Isles, in Shetland, Orkney and north-east Caithness.

Seahouses women were contracted by fish merchants to process the herring, usually the salting into barrels which formed the great bulk of the trade They were recruited in 'crews' of 3; 2 to gut; 1 to pack, each alternating around so there was not a heap lying waiting to be packed. Some Seahouses women were at Baltasound on Unst in the Shetlands only 179 miles from Norway. My mother and her sisters used to go to the mainland ports of Scrabster and Thurso, the long journey by train arranged and paid for by their employer. There were no fixed wages as such, payment being made on the number of barrels packed until they were full. After a few days the salt herring sank down some inches so they had to be topped up again. When I was a small boy I used to help my mother by doing this chore for her. A Seahouses crew held the record for number of barrels packed in one day. If I remember rightly it was 24, but how many working hours this represented, I do not know. It was a messy job often done in the open without shelter. They had to be tough to stand the conditions as the salt was coarse and strong and a cut finger, of which there were many, was slow to heal and agony when the salt got in. They had to wear finger cloots because the speed the gutters worked at it was easy to get a cut somewhere on the hands. They wore a uniform of sorts – long skirts of tweed, heavy boots, a skirt and bib of oilskin and a woollen shawl over the head and shoulders.

Accomodation was also made available by their employers, maybe lodging with local people, sometimes in nothing better than wooden huts. They cooked for themselves; their belongings in wooden 'kists' about 3 feet long by 18 inches broad by 16 inches deep. These were their own property and often deputised for seats or beds.

If a wife was expecting a child she did not go to the far fishings but did go to the home one when it came on. When the child was born and weaned it was taken by its mother to the yard where she worked so she could look after its needs. As the home fishing was during the warmer months of the year this was no hardship for the little one. There was a large stock of new, empty barrels always on hand usually stowed under an open fronted shed for easy access. They were made of soft white pine, the insides singed by the coopers in forming them and they had a peculiar pleasant tangy smell Many a time I have seen mother's little joy well wrapped in woollen shawls tucked into a waist high barrel (they were always stored on their sides) and snoring away contentedly while mother was packing a few feet away.

As was the custom in those early days, large families were the rule, and as the lads went in the family boats they had usually a sister or two to bait their lines until marriageable age. But crewing the boats by families was not a good idea for, if a boat was lost, one family lost at least most or all of its male members. On the other hand it was also a harsh introduction to the laddie just starting his sea career. A lot of men had not the time to spend showing the lad the proper way to do things, because in a boat of only 3 or 4 hands there was not much time to spare when working the gear, and anyone not capable of pulling their weight made it proportionately harder for the others. But you learned quickly, I'll say that much, and you never made the same mistake twice. The foregoing figures for crews apply to the smaller boats or cobles. Many of the herring boats were large, heavy boats capable of carrying a lot of fish. They needed more men to handle them, some had 8 or 9 or even more of a crew yet often there was a shortage of manpower to crew the whole fleet, so they took extra hands in the shape of casual labourers of all sorts. Irish lads over here for the potato and corn harvests used to come a few months early and sign on. They were known as 'half sharemen' because the earnings were shared out by the crew, the boat receiving a share, the crew a share each whilst the 'half sharemen' got a half since they did not contribute any gear. Each regular fisherman provided his own share of nets. When the big keelboats went to the 'back-end' fishing at Yarmouth they had all local crews for then the small boats, being too small or old, were left behind and their crews doubled up in the big ones.

At this point I would like to explain that our name 'keelboat' refers to the type of double ended boats that were originally built on or about the Firth of Forth and which in their time were common among other models all down the Scottish coast and the north east of England. Quite a lot were worked from Yorkshire ports but there was also another type of east coast design, so it was the Yorkshire coast where the 'keelboat' design ended. In recent years there has been an upsurge of interest in old fishing craft and several books have been written on the subject. In most I have come across there seems to be some confusion over the name 'keel boat' and they are calling this type 'fifies'. There seems to be misunderstanding in that, as far as fishing went, Northumberland was only an extension of the Scottish coast, except that, owing to the nature of the Northumbrian coast, the inshore fishing was done from the distinctive cobles. The herring boats were known as 'keelboats' from the Firth of Forth to Yorkshire – it was the more northerly Scotsmen who called them 'Fifies'.

While on this subject I want to point out some misconceptions. 'Keelboats' and 'cobles' are entirely different types of boat. The former is self–explanatory. They had a long, *deep,* keel making them extremely fast under sail and able to carry a great of canvas. I imagine that confusion arises with the River Tyne 'Keels'. These were small barges that used to load the old coalships. The old Tyneside song 'Weel may the keel row......' refers to them.

I will be dealing with the more technical aspects of keelboats and cobles later so, in the meantime, I'll get back to the annals of the village.

Seahouses was never recognised by writers as the important herring port it was. Many casually dismissed it along with the lesser villages as of no consequence. In fact, at the peak of the herring years, there were 10 herring yards going full blast, not counting the packing going on on every available piece of spare ground. In the 1880s it had assumed such importance that the harbour was extended considerably. A long pier and a breakwater were built and the inner harbour was altered by modifying what is now the middle pier. Prior to that the middle pier had been the outer one. Over 300 boats landed herring daily, boats coming from all over England and Scotland – Cornishmen from St.Ives; Manxmen from Peel; others from all the eastern Scottish ports. At the weekends they crowded the harbour, the surplus having to go to Holy Island or Beadnell. Like the herring boat crews there were not enough local lasses to work the herring so the girls arrived from as far away as the Outer Hebrides. There were even crews of lasses from Holy Island. The village was literally bursting at the seams, the shopkeepers all benefitting from the bonanza. Local farmers hired out lorries and horses to haul the catches to the yards. There was no need to hunt for a job!. True, the wages were not much then, but folks were content with what they got; they adapted to that way of life and thought nothing of it. There was no trouble. Some of the visiting fishermen had a noggin or two in the local pubs but in the main they were a decent hard–working lot of men.

The 'Speedwell', the last keelboat out of Seahouses. It had two Kelvin 26-30 engines, and no wheelhouse. The owners were Chas. Dawson and family. The date is late 1920s.

There was no fishing on the Sabbath with the week finishing on the Saturday, fairly late, if landings were heavy, the boats making seawards again on Monday. Neither was there any bad language – women were respected and treated accordingly. There were liaisons and, obviously, lasses and lads courted and married.

The fishing community was one great family all down the east coast and you could not go into any port without somebody of your acquaintance hailing you.

Mechanisation was on the move, steam capstans were installed in the larger 55/60 feet keel boats, mainly to haul nets, but also as they could be used to set the enormous foresails.

There was a very neat set up, with the capstan on the starboard quarter just aft of the mizzen. Its engine was in an iron casing with the 6 feet boiler standing upright under the deck. This needed stoking and topping up with water only now and again. The main hauling apparatus was a cage circulating around the body of the machine, with a small fast pulley wheel projecting outside the engine casing to take care of the discharging side.

About the late 1890s there arrived the first steam driven drifter, at first merely a converted sailing smack of the East Anglian model, which was the subsequent design for those custom built ones that followed. Early boilers were vertical with the top projecting through the deck. The steering was open tiller with auxiliary sails being carried. Wheel- houses were added, initially on the after side of the funnel, later models had them placed fore side of the funnel.

Steam drifters rang the death-knell of the sailing boats. They could not compete with the boats that could get to sea, fish, and land their catches with regularity, no longer dependent on the whims of the winds. Building yards of England and Scotland were ringing with the sound of saws, caulking hammers and riveters building steam drifters. Owners of new or nearly new sailing boats were looking at the newly produced internal combustion engines which by 1905 were starting to appear in the Scottish fleet. These were fairly easy to install and, while now may appear to have been of insufficient horse power, they seemed then to be quite adequate and drove the vessel at a moderate speed. The crew could still hoist sails to help them along.

Steam drifters were not owned at Seahouses as, unlike their Scottish cousins, they did not pursue the herring all year round. Just before 1914 they was only one keelboat motorised. The 60 feet 'Margaret Dawson' was owned by the Dawson family who also had the 'Speedwell', the only keelboat left after the first war. This was smaller with twin 26-30 flat sump Kelvin paraffin engines. She was used prior to the second war before being scrapped or sold.

I can remember being taken down into the cabin of our family keel boat, the 'Father and Sons', Reg.No. BK432, a sailer then. That would be about early summer 1914, when I'd be getting on for 3 years old. I remember it still, standing by myself in the cabin while they set up the mizzen mast. Like the rest of the fleet of big boats she was sold away, I don't know where. I saw her once more about 1919 or 1920 going south under power after her new owners had installed an oil engine. A few boats that were not sold were laid up in the creek at Waren Mill all through the war, but in time they also went. One, the Euphemia, which belonged to my uncle William Donaldson, Senr., was broken up on the beach at Seahouses harbour. During the war the fishermen who were not on naval service fished for white fish and shell fish from the two types of cobles operating on the coast.

When the war finished some big mules (sharp sterned cobles) were purchased at Burnmouth, just north of Berwick, and converted to motor. Usually the conversions were to the simple uncomplicated paraffin engines, the Kelvins as they were called, made at Glasgow by the Bergious Company. Funnily enough they started off by making motor cars at the beginning of the century, switching later to marine engines.

In the Great Depression of the 1920s things were in a parlous state as many European, especially German, outlets for the British salt herring export failed. The herring industry suffered terribly. Britain could not absorb the quantity of herring caught so there was great hardship. Many successful skippers went bankrupt. Men had to leave the sea; boats were lying idle, costing harbour dues and fees for maintenance; thus dwindling their owners hard wrought capital away. Many whose owners could no longer afford the expenses were towed out of the harbours and allowed to drift ashore as wrecks to be smashed up by the sea.

When things started to look rosier a year or two into the 1930s it was with a sadly depleted fleet. Some new experimental boats were designed and built with Government grants, but only a very limited number. Here at Seahouses the fleet of smaller boats managed to survive by reason of their low running costs and the introduction of the seine nets used mostly for flat fish at first. It was a Danish invention which caught on rapidly on the south Firth of Forth ports and the small keelboats of 30–38 feet, called 'Yolls', were adapted to work it. Eventually some of them landed here to try our local grounds. The net could only be operated on very smooth, sandy grounds but it was an instant success with hefty landings of prime plaice the order of the day. After crewing up with the Forth men to get experience, several of the local men, including my family, fit out for working the new gear. Some years previously all the local boats had been fitted with a 'hauler' driven off the main engine and placed either in the bows of the double ended boats or aft in the cobles to enable the shell fishing gear, the creaves, to be worked more easily. It was a simple mushroom shaped cast iron wheel with a deep niche to grip the rope around its outside circumference. As the seine net required two ropes to operate, another wheel was bolted to the top of the first one and the thing was done. Things did not proceed as merrily as the proverbial marriage bell however. There were few ports on this coast capable of being used by the deeper draught boats which were better for operating the net. Cobles were too light to work it successfully and, as the new method caught on, those who could not work it wanted it stopped altogether. They could not perceive that times were changing again as had happened in the past. One old Craster fisherman declared that the decline of the inshore fishing was due to the internal combustion engine!. The south shore Firthers had the same reaction from their counterparts on the north shore. Prophets of doom were declaiming that all the fish would be cleaned up in no time at all. I should at this point explain that for 3 miles offshore around the coasts was an exclusion zone supposedly the breeding grounds of the seas supply of fish!

A campaign of opposition was mounted against the Seahouses men. Not all of those who took part or aired their views in the papers had ever caught a fish in their lives. Rumours were circulated that this new method had caught salmon!. In fact anything was permissible to discredit the seine–net and to hint that the 'sacred cow' of coastal fish –the salmon –being caught was enough to cause an uproar. That uproar still continues in a way but now directed into another channel – the coastal salmon fishers – men who all their lives and those of their forefathers for generations back have followed the salmon fishing for their livelihood. They now in their turn are being persecuted by other powerful groups. The villain of the piece is now the mono–filament net. It seems that nothing alters. By the beginning of Hitler's war legislation had been passed by the Northumbrian Sea Fisheries Committee to restrict the seine net inside the three mile limit to four months each year: March, August, September, October. The most unproductive months of the year were selected when fish were scarce. Cod and haddock circulate in quantities during the winter months and again in late spring and summer. The open times were selected so that when the fish were on the grounds they had to be caught in the late spring and summer by hand line and in the winter by the long line method, surely the most energy and time consuming method ever devised for its unfortunate users!. Long lining meant that the whole family had to muck in and help while the returns at the end of the week never reimbursed the operators with the money they had worked for. It was a form of slavery. What the opponents of the seine net ignored deliberately or otherwise was that in the total area of ground between say, Holy Island and Dunstanburgh Castle, the only ground capable of using the seine net amounted to less than 10%. 90% was hard rock.

Came the war and unrestricted fishing was the order of the day. Things were never the same again even more so than at the end of the first world war.

From the early 1920s onwards, even in the depression years, every summer saw families from the towns, mostly Tyneside but also Edinburgh and Glasgow, coming to spend a week or two at the seaside. Most arrived by train at Chathill, coming to Seahouses by the local line with the green-painted 'Bamburgh' locomotive pulling the three passenger coaches. Some went to the hotels but the majority of mainly working class folks were accomodated by local families in their spare rooms. To the local housewives it was a help to the exchequer. Charges were modest, seldom more than £2.00 per week. Meals were provided in this charge —and I mean real meals —no skimping in quantity, if somewhat plain in quality. Real Northumbrian Border hospitality!. Being absorbed into a fishing community was a new experience for the visitor; a way of life undreamed of in the 'brick canyons' where they lived and worked. They came pale faced and departed with a healthy tan and looking like different people. Their days were usually spent on the beaches taking a snack with them to eat at midday, returning to their lodgings about 5 or 6 pm to their main meal of the day. Most of the boats ran to the Farnes when they could pick up a few people. The trip would last as long as 3 or 4 hours for about 5/- (25p) a head and a limit of 12 passengers per boat.

It was not uncommon to see artists sitting sketching the harbour, some really good. Sir William Russell Flint, the famous artist stayed at the Ship Hotel one summer. Several of his water colours had the local sands as backgrounds to his studies of nudes.

I got quite pally with his son who was about my age. This was the start of the 'touristi horrende' age and the local council, then based at Belford, got fair bemused by it, devoting much time and thought to promoting it. The village had not altered or increased much during the previous years and the lifeboat house was still in the square where the Dolphin restaurant now stands. In 1935 the new boat- house was built down the north bank to house the new motor life- boat, the 35 ft. Watson type, the W.R.A.

About this time the old village smithy, originally a 'but-and-ben' type of cottage run by a local man named Davy Cormack, stood between the access to the Bamburgh Castle Hotel and where the Dolphin's west wall is. The 'powers that be' declared it an eyesore. It was the sort of thing they drool over nowadays It should have been made a listed building, standing proudly today as 'Ye Old Village Smithy' complete with plastic hammers and horseshoes, no doubt. The upshot was that poor Davy was chucked out willy-nilly and the cottage demolished. The ground was really then an eyesore, I can tell you, and remained so for years. Had it been put to local opinion it would have been difficult to have found 2 or 3 people in a 10 mile radius who found it an 'eyesore'.

At length we have arrived at the Hitler's war era. Local builders were employed making large concrete cubes along the sands where it was supposed a sea-borne invasion could be mounted. Most yet remain. After a spell of trepidation things went into a groove again. At a recruiting drive which I attended a lot of lads signed up for the Army, the Territorials, I think. We fishermen were told we were earmarked for the Navy. Most of the lads who signed on that evening were captured by the Japs at Singapore. Occasionally there were alarms. Several ships in convoy were blown up outside of the Longstone, the crews of two such, the Norwegian 'Pluto' and the British 'Baltanglia', were picked up by Seahouses boats and brought ashore. Minesweepers, converted fishing steam trawlers, used to anchor inside of the inner islands.

Then Dunkirk, and we were on stand-by, but it was deemed too far and too late for us to get there in time to help with the evacuation. Fish prices jumped and species that had been unwanted, mackerel for example, were in big demand. In early and midsummer 1940 an enormous quantity of mackerel was seen in our waters. Never before or since has there been anything like it. From Holy Island head to Beadnell Point the sea was literally chock full of large mackerel. They could be seen easily in the clear water under the boat. My uncle and I went fishing for them in our small coble using mackerel flies on gut, made from gulls white feathers on haddock hooks. Often the four hooks on the cast were barely into the water when they were seized by the fish just under the surface. I had got my calling-up papers for the Navy so I was glad to be able to make a few extra pounds before going into the minesweepers where the pay was microscopic.

When I returned in 1945 it was to a very different village. Everybody was preoccupied with their own problems. The returning fishermen found their gear had rotted or had been eaten full of holes by rats. The Inland Revenue would only allow relief for gear bought *after I commenced earning*, no relief being granted for the weeks and months getting the pieces together. Those who had been at home, too old or rejected for service, had spent their earnings on larger boats for seine or drift fishing or ring net herring fishing.

Seine net herring fishing operated successfully for a lot of years along with the ring net for herring, a method evolved by the Clyde fishermen.

As shoals of herring had proliferated during the war years the old cycle was again to the fore with herring mid and late summer into September. The west coast boats were handsome, canoe-sterned craft, all varnish and silver paint, more like yachts than fishing boats, often with Gaelic names, 'Morag Mhor', etc., came and filled the inner harbour from side to side. There was a feeling of rejuvenation in the village; things were as they should be, a fishing village running at full blast. The revival was to vanish in a few short years, but what a time while it lasted!. Old friendships were renewed, new ones made, one happy brotherhood of the sea.

Behind it lay disaster. It was all just a facade for the yards had long ceased to be operational, the buyers had died out or grown old, and the herring were carted off in 40 gallon drums on big lorries to the fish-meal factories for cattle food. The transport system failed sometimes and the boats that came in in the morning choc-a-block with herrings did not get them out until evening.

In the meantime a little cloud was making its presence felt in northern waters. A new type of net appeared, the mid water herring trawl, capable of adjustment to fish at any depth the fish were lying. There was no escape for the herrings day or night and, to hasten the final end, the Icelandic Government subsidised a new method called purse-seining for herring. This was the most horrific means of destruction yet and eventually it cleaned up the shoals almost to extinction. So much for the herring!.

The former seine netters here then started trawling with the otter trawl, the method used by the big steam trawlers in Arctic waters. These nets were capable of being worked over semi-hard ground so more and more areas were swept ruthlessly. Another modification came about, the Rock-hopper trawl, which speaks for itself. Fitted with large rubber rollers on the sole-rope of the net, it can travel over all but the most foul ground. Finally, with virtually everybody at it, the fish almost vanished and the young men who worked as crew left to take work ashore. Boats were sold and not replaced. The fleet shrank to about half the strength it had been and the ones that were left scratched a bare existence. The smaller boats turned to shell fishing and a half dozen custom built launches worked on the Farne Islands passenger trade during the summer.

This, then, is the story of the Seahouses and North Sunderland. The village by the sea – hemmed in on both sides by two large caravan sites – the village that is no longer a fishing community. Like the rest of our coastal villages it is where the old Norse-accented tongue is dying out and where a way of life is lost forever. The old close knit atmosphere lives no more; the natives scattered and spread out in the Council-built 'reservation' in the village, somehow apart from it, a village within a village.

The story of the people and their way of life for centuries, the people whom I have heard described as 'ignorant' and 'peasants' by people who, in a different strata of society, thought they were superior. 'Peasants' they undoubtedly were, 'ignorant' they may have been. But they were people who, not only in Northumberland, but all around the British coast, lived out their lives and were content with what they got. Who only deserved to be left alone to get on with their own business. Who out of pity for others manned the lifeboats, sometimes losing their own lives in the process, and who sought no reward except the satisfaction of a job well done. Compare them to the men of science who have devoted their many talents to their discoveries and who have succeeded in producing more and more efficient and horrible ways of destroying their fellow men. What an achievment! Weighed in the balance, who then is the better man? They lived with nature in their daily tasks like the farm worker through whose efforts the rest of peoples'

29

stomachs were filled. As man in his blind ignorance departs further
and further from nature, so he is sowing seeds he will finally
reap.

> 'With Earth's first clay, they did the last mans knead,
> And then of the Last Harvest sowed the seed,
> Yea, the first Morning of Creation wrote,
> What the last Dawn of Reckoning shall read!'

.........so said **Omar**.

If I perhaps have stressed the fishing aspect a bit too strongly I make
no apology. I was born of a very long line of seamen and fishermen, indeed my birthplace was only a matter of a few yards from
salt water, my infant eyes gazing on a forest of masts, and my ears
beguiled by the click-click rattle of the block sheaves when the
sails were hoisted.
What follows is a mixture of facts, opinions, anecdotes, explanations
and whatever. If it opens a few windows on us, as we were, I'll
be satisfied.

3.   THE SPOKEN WORD.

What I have jaloused for a number of years is that we Border
Northumbrians are in danger of losing that most precious possession
 - our unique manner of speech.
I am not going to fall into the trap of trying to determine the roots
of the tongue because I believe it is not a dialect as much as the
remains of an older language. In it the 'Y' sound is much to the
fore- 'hyem; tyek; byekin'- in English, home, take, baking.
Northumberland is triangular in shape, the east bordered by the
North Sea, the west by the English-Scottish border, the south by the
Tyne. Within that large triangle we have at least three main
versions of the spoken tongue; were it possible to produce a written
version, it would come out fairly common to the three in context.
There are many words common with Lowland Scots, not
surprisingly, but many have an affinity with Old Norse, several
examples having only a letter or two switched round.
When we went to school none of us bairns could speak 'proper'
English, as it was quaintly called. Our teachers used to make us

30

mouth the words over and over to pronounce them, so we were, in effect, bi-lingual, with English as she is spoke being our second tongue. The girls adapted quicker than us boys and somehow there was a feeling that to 'taak broad' was 'common' for some reason – maybe a mild form of snobbery. It resulted in some ludicrous and funny situations, like the lassie who, on a trip to the Farnes in her father's boat, said to a lady who had jostled her accidentally on disembarking, 'pardon me, madam, but ye've struppen on me fut!' There was also the lady who had a sister married and living in London. Returning home from a holiday with her sister, she had managed to 'get her tongue sandpapered', in other words a spurious London accent. Her neighbours were a bit put out by her show-off until one day she made a gaffe when one of them, admiring her new gloves was told, 'yerss, they're rawther naice, but they've one bed fault. When they start to go, they gaan aaltigither!

If you imagine a broad swathe of country south of a line from say Alnmouth through Alnwick on to Corbridge and Hexham. Before the northward drift of the southerners began, the general speech was spoken in much the same manner. Between Amble and the Tyne another accent predominated, and on Tyneside itself came the true 'Geordie' twang. Nothing annoys me more than to be told that because I'm a Northumbrian, I am therefore a 'Geordie'. There is a great difference between the 'Geordie' speech and Border-Northumbrian. We pronounce our 'R's, which, they do not. Maybe they did speak like us in the past but now it is a hybrid tongue, brought into being, perhaps, by trying to speak reasonable English. In so doing they have managed to eliminate the 'R' completely – 'she took a cheh(chair) upstehs(upstairs), combed her feh heh(fair hair) and got a peh(pair) of stockings to cover her beh(bare) legs!.

From Amble south it is a sharp accent but the double 'O's are strongly emphasised. We say 'gan doon' for 'going down'; they will say 'gan' or 'gannen dooon', long drawn out 'oo' sound or 'aam no varry weeel' (I'm not very well). The Border strip covers a lot of territory and, while not heavily populated, is consistent in speech. At Kielder, 70 miles south west of Seahouses, there were only a few words spoken differently. How do I know?. My wife came from there! Within this area of basically common speech, there could be differences in the pronounciation of words between nearby

31

villages. I heard a Craster native talking about a 'cyort'(a cart) while 8 miles north at Seahouses it is pronounced 'cairt' in the Scots fashion. North Tyne speech at Kielder in our father's time produced 'stee-an' (stone) but at Seahouses, it was 'styen'. In some of the pit villages 'chain' would be said as such; in the next place it would be 'chine'. Puzzling to the southerner to say the least!. The natives of Holy Island had a distinctive speech of their own with an affinity to some areas up south Tweedside.

One thing making me cringe is the account of how Hotspur, when at the English court was thought to 'have a defect in his speech, and, being a folk hero, his fellow countrymen copied the way he spoke' How could one man so influence the whole of the Northumbrians when it is probable that most never saw him in their lives, let alone heard him speak!

I find it almost impossible to speak entirely in Northumbrian with a non-native.   With another native, yes, the conversation flows smoothly.   Speaking to an English speaker, I realise subconsciously that he is not following all of my speech, so I tend to use English thereafter in the complicated sentences!.

A true tale happened in 1940 when two Holy Island brothers, a Boulmer lad, half a dozen from Newbiggin by the Sea and me were landed at Lowestoft after an overnight train journey. A Navy lorry transported us to the naval depot at the 'Nest', a former open air concert hall and area. We were talking in a group, noting the busy aspect of the place and wondering when we would be directed somewhere. The large English Chief Petty Officer who had been standing alongside us suddenly said, in very careful English, 'join your friends over there', at the same time pointing to a group across at the other side. The Newbiggin lad to whom he spoke said 'we have no friends here, we're strangers', whereupon the CPO said, 'aren't you Norwegians?'. Now it was exactly as it was written, so take it or leave it – and that was only the start!.

Having passed various tests and firing the regulation 3 shots at a paper target with a worn out Boer War rifle to prove I knew which end was which, I was rated 'Able Seaman'. Able to 'hand, reef and steer' in the old parlance, I could hand and steer but reefing was out as Nelson's sailing Navy was long since gone. After a few days in which we got kitted out we were drafted to various ports. I landed at Grimsby, a main east coast minesweeping centre. After various ships and adventures I was admitted to hospital with a nasty form of poisoning, I know not what. When I eventually started to take an interest in my surroundings and fellow patients, I discovered to my pleasure that the lad on my right was, like myself, a fisherman, but from Campbeltown. At the foot of our beds another contained a Norwegian sailor about 40 years old. He was called Trygve, his surname I cannot remember. One day I had been talking at some length to the Kintyre lad when Trygve suddenly said in fluent English, 'Andrew, are you British?, I replied, 'aye, why do you ask?'. 'Where do you come from?', he asked. 'From a little fishing village south of Berwick', I said. 'Does everybody there speak the same as you?', he asked, 'because I know your friend is a Scot, but when you speak to him in your own language, if I did'nt know any English, I could understand most of what you say!' To say I was flabbergasted would be to put it lightly. To the amusement of the Kintyre lad, Trygve and I started comparing, but he said my speech was Old Norse. I made a point after that when passing a Norwegian destroyer, the 'Draug' (Dragon), I'd speak to the crew I knew in broad Northumbrian, much to their amusement!.

'Whor commer de fra?' – Norwegian.
'Whor d'ye cum fra?' – Northumbrian.

'Home' in English is 'hyem' in Old Norse, 'hjem' in modern Norwegian; and 'hyem' in Northumbrian.

Among the southern English we are invariably Scots. So much for speech!.
But what about the Northumbrian character?.. At least one writer got very annoyed with us. Neither the name of the book nor the author can I recall but I do remember the paragraph in which he castigated us. He wrote that no matter on which subject he talked, or what he had seen and experienced, some Northumbrians would come out with a tale of what he or somebody else had seen or done more than the listener had! I've known that happen. I am sure this is a character defect arising from a desire for independence. An inability in a lot of natives outlook to accept another viewpoint! Something very potent has to occur to make them all 'spit on one stone' as they so elegantly put it!. There is a deep rooted desire for Jack to be as good as his master and I feel that same flaw caused us to lose our country all those years ago. A fatal weakness.

'For those behind cried, 'Forward',
And those in front cried,'back'!

At the same time the Northumbrian is a friendly person. Though sometimes unfairly blamed as being uncooperative, silent and strange it is more often that the visitor will ignore him and so never realises that he would like to be approached first. Ostentatious people and posturings were frowned upon, a brash person being castigated as 'afaa forritsome'. Despite travelling to other ports and places, the fishing people at least, would not concede that any way of life was better than their own! They endeavoured to avoid the limelight, the glare of publicity was not to their liking at all. They took a lot of convincing to accept anything new. Changes had to take place slowly, to be tested and evaluated before coming into general being.

They were individuals, only acting in concert when needful. They could be led, but not driven, hated to be 'talked down to', formed their own opinions, sticking doggedly to them come hell or high water, in fact a right stubborn lot. They had a lot of Norse ancestry in their make–up. A little parable to illustrate the point. One of my forebears, a long time ago, owned a coble with another. They fell out over something, probably a triviality, enough to arouse a passionate disagreement, whereupon one of the twain took a saw and cut the boat in half, leaving each with a piece of useless timber only fit to convert to a henhouse!. A village community then was like one large family and like ordinary families there were squabbles soon resolved, but sometimes the parties sulked for quite a long time. To their credit they are capable of great compassion, a death affecting the whole community. On the funeral day blinds in neighbours' houses were drawn respectfully. Funerals were usually well attended as the deceased would be known to all. Now, some of my life–long acquaintances have been dead and buried before I knew!. There was always help for the bereaved if only in contact sympathetically.

That deep down they were capable of strong emotions is illustrated by the fact that in the early 1860s, Miss Skelly, heiress to the lime business, was wed to a Dr.Belaney who had a practice in London. They lived at Seafield Farm, now a service complex for the caravan park. Dr.Belaney had high flown plans to rejuvenate the quarries, which had been allowed to run to seed. When in London his wife was poisoned under mysterious circumstances and an attempt made to blame suicide. The Doctor was charged in court but acquitted on lack of evidence. That there had been some queer goings-on was undeniable. Local people were convinced she had been the victim of foul play. When Belaney returned here, there was a riot, the locals running him out. He was last seen running up over the old Iron Age graveyard, disappearing westward, never to return. The house was looted and set on fire. An elderly woman fell over the wall of the Ha-ha with an armful of china!. The locals were charged with riotous assembly, looting, and arson, many appearing at Belford court. Magistrates must have had misgivings about the Doctor, for most cases were dismissed, and the ring leaders given small fines.

Another instance occurred several decades later and concerned a small German sailing ship in the harbour. The cabin boy, about 13 or 14 years old, was systematically 'ill-used' by the Captain. This was soon noticed by the locals and a fund put together at the instigation of the fishermens' wives – most of whom could ill afford it. The lad was removed from the ship forcibly, taken to Chathill, put on a train to the German Consulate on the Tyne, and sent home to Germany!.

In my teens, the 'Argo', from Eyemouth, was towed into Seahouses in a sudden gale in a sinking condition. The crew were soaked to the skin and suffering from hypothermia. Minutes after landing they were hustled off to the nearest fishermens' homes, given warm, dry clothes, food, and looked after, no return being sought. These are just two instsances, countless others went unrecorded. What a contrast to the 'I'm alright, Jack' brigade. Helping each other was common among the coast people.

Departing from these shores for a wee while to Whitehills, a fishing village, a mile from Banff. Many years ago a Norwegian ship was lost with all hands just east of the present harbour. She was laden with coal which was washed ashore when she broke up. The locals collected and sold all they could, the proceeds being sent to the crews' dependents in Norway. Like their Northumbrian cousins, they were dirt poor, but strove their best and more to help people even worse off. Blood is thicker than water; the ancient Norse strain runs strong up the coast.

To be a member of a fishing community has gained me an entree

Our family keelboat taken about 1914. Left to right are Richard Allen Jnr; John Rutter, the Author's father; Henry Allen; Wm.Rutter, grandfather. Robert Rutter is up the mast. The Author's mother was from the Allen family.

into a special society. This has been my experience many times through life. *'Hae ye been a fisherman?'* The open sesame. I cannot describe it for it is unlike any other emotion I know. It is to be part of the Brotherhood of the Sea.

4.   OF VISITORS AND BOATS..........

I must be forgiven if my writing is liberally splashed with sea water. I was a fisherman and as a fisherman I write. It would be presumptious of me to write about farming, of which I know so little. I can describe a boat, but never a horse. To me it is a large animal with a long head, chunky body and a leg at each corner, the finer points eluding me entirely. When during these past 30 years or so I have come across writers describing the coastal fishing boats I have come to the conclusion that many know as much about them as I know about horses!. When coming across some of the errors in the description of boats that I know well, I wonder if the descriptions of boats of which I've only a slight knowledge is 100% correct either!.

The emergence of glass fibre as a boat building material has produced some weird effects. I do not consider them as 'boats' and the kindest thing I can say about them is that they float. While some have made some sleek hulls amongst the sailers, I view the majority of power craft as 'abominations on water'. 'By gosh', you say, 'that's a bit strong, isn't it?', but I'm only exercising my right as a Northumbrian to say what I think. For a start, glass fibre is an artifical product spawned in a laboratory, lacking affinity with nature. It is as soulless as anything you can imagine. Back in the days when men first conceived the idea of making a watertight wooden box with sharp ends, there has been a mystique, a magical quality, if you like, about the whole set up. Men trusted their lives on a frightening and dangerous element in a wooden shell and it was no accident that the shell was imbued with a life of its own. The trees that supplied the wood had a life within them; the same life had flowed through the fibres of the planks under their hands and feet. The very movement of the water imparted movement to the boat, so they came to regard it with special affection. They gave it a pet name and painted eyes on it so that she could find her way in the dark. This happened world wide and was not confined to any one part as men came to this conclusion everywhere.

So for centuries the boat or ship was made of natural materials, driven by oars or by sails spread to the wind. Time was spent making them beautiful and their crews delighted in their appearance. As time went by new methods and models arrived. Larger ships appeared which in the northern world were built in their own distinctive way – the clench or overlapping plank method – the model, a double-ended vessel with high bow and stem, breadth proportionate to the length, the motive power oars, and the universal square sail.

In the fullness of time the Norsemen had evolved some remarkable inventions. They had a great affinity with the sea and their vessels were designed to ride the water in the best possible manner. They had a strong poetic streak in them. They termed the sea the 'Swan's Bath', and their vessels had imaginative names like 'Sea Maiden', 'Bride of the Ware'(seaweed), Sea Bear', Odin's Pride', etc. They were so involved with all things pertaining to the sea and ships that even their houses were similarly shaped. One such boatshaped ruin has been unearthed on the high Yorkshire Fells. That they had a strong concept of the rightness of their ships can be seen in the following tale from the Norse Sagas, the wonderful semi–historical accounts that give us a detailed insight into how they lived and worked all those years ago. It goes thus, as far as I can remember, although in some accounts the names are spelled differently.

A certain King ordered a new ship to be built for himself by the foremost builder of the day, no expense spared. His name has been given as Thorfin Skarfhogg. In due course the ship was completed and the launching day arranged. Meantime all who had watched her in building were unanimous in declaring that never had they beheld such a handsome vessel. She was a thing of grace and beauty. She would be gone over inch by inch by the old men, who were very stern critics indeed, but no fault could be found. Came the great day of the launch! The king, with his retinue, was early at the ship and to their horror found that, overnight, someone had cut several deep notches along the upper plank on one side. Naturally the king was in a towering rage, declaring to all and sundry that the person who had committed such an almost sacreligious deed would suffer death. Whereupon out stepped old Thorfin, no doubt hiding a grin beneath his beard, declaring to the king, 'you'll have to kill me then, for it was I who did it'. The onlookers were flabbergasted, and when the king asked why, Thorfin said, 'look!', and taking his shipwright's axe, he trimmed the plank down until the cuts were eliminated. All agreed that, if possible, the alteration had made the ship even more beautiful!.

Now these were men who, centuries ago, with primitive hand tools, thought out and produced efficient sea-going vessels, whose construction has been so well described many times that there is no need for me to duplicate it. The existing examples of the Gokstad and Oseberg ships are there for all to see. No slide rules or computers were used by the builders in their design. With the instinct of wild things they arrived subconsciously at the best way to proceed. The Mediterranian Sea was where the other form of construction, the carvel or smooth-planked ship, was evolved. Both methods produced sturdy sea-going vessels and the basic underwater lines of the old Norse ships have lasted until recent years. The Keelboats, Scaffies, and Zulus of the northern coast of Britain are similar to the longships. Look at the old keelboats at the shore at Holy Island, now doing duty as fishermens' stores.

No two wooden boats were ever built exactly alike, consequently each had individual characteristics peculiarly their own. One would be easy to row but awkward under sail, another the opposite. The feel of a boat underfoot was often an indication of her qualities.

Some were 'tender' i.e. feeling a bit unstable, some firm and steady. Anyone associated with small boats from an early age will know what I mean. Again, while the eye may look over a number of boats without great interest, there will be one that strikes the beholder with considerable force. Something about her will appeal to the imagination, generating a desire to own her, even though it is unfulfilled. While the power boat amateur sailor who tears about over the water in his plastic runabout (they even have to resemble a motor car in interior layout) powered by an outboard motor imagines he is proving something, he will never acquire seamanship in this manner, even if he does it all his life.

To be a real seaman you've got to start at the bottom of the scale because the sea cannot, and will not, be played with. It must be treated with the utmost respect. It is much larger, more powerful, unpredictable and dangerous than the average landsman suspects.

You see them in the summer, with their flashy outfits, launching down the beach, often unaware that the tide is ebbing faster than they are preparing so they get into the soft sand at the old pier end. People who are so contemptuous of local advice and of the sea should not be allowed to go outside the breakwater. This tale illustrates what I mean. Four or five years ago on a Saturday there came a party of anglers with three tow boats behind their cars. As it was very foggy the harbour was closed by the Harbourmaster and no launchings allowed. They went eight miles down the coast to Craster where no such instructions applied, and launched, I did hear, against local advice. The fog must have been a trifle thinner there, but it soon thickened and they had to be rescued. I happened to glance through a publication for sea anglers and was struck by a caption 'Super Cool Anglers'. It went on to describe how a party of anglers in three cobles!!? were caught in a fog off the dangerous Northumbrian coast. Rather than risk going through dangerous reefs, they radioed for help. As the Seahouses lifeboat inched its way through fog, they calmly carried on fishing and caught more fish. Now in spite of all the advice given to them, they still persisted in putting out to sea, knowing they would be searched for if they got into trouble. They were not in any of trouble from a fisherman's point of view; there was no sea on. It was calm, just foggy. Conditions that fishermen would take in their daily stride. The fact was that they were so incompetent that they could not find the mainland of Britain half a mile away. The fact that they had a ship to shore radio meant that they were meaning to use it to get help even before they set out. The lifeboat did not inch its way to them, it had to belt at full speed, finding them on radar at the same time. Had a more serious mishap occurred at the Farne Islands at the same time, the lifeboat would have been sorely tried to attend both calls. The magazine article was making them almost heroes. Now there are the 'know-it-alls', the clever ones, the ones who blame a 'freak wave', if they are capsized or whatever. People who behave like that should be made to pay the expenses of their rescue. These people come to play, I cannot find an alternative word, and frankly they are a damned nuisance. While any idiot can go out to sea in unsuitable craft the motorist has to pass a stringent test both to his fitness to drive and the mechanical condition of his vehicle.

Some of the articles brought here purporting to be boats have proved the foregoing to be correct. A dozen or so years ago, it would be midsummer, I had been along to the pier end lighthouse. I saw one of these 'plastic frogs' nosing out from behind the middle pier end. It was about 12 feet long or less, shaped like an arrow head, with an enormous outboard motor capable, I'd say, of driving a 40 or 50 foot boat nae bother. In some peoples reasoning, the bigger the motor the faster you go, irrespective of the suitability of the float. As I say, here it came, creeping out, the sole occupant looking this way and that to see if all was clear, as it was. Suddenly, and I mean suddenly, he must have opened full out (I forgot to say the 'boat' had about 4 inches of water aft). The propellor dug in at full revs, the craft literally stood on end vertically, and promptly sank with the weight of the enormous engine. The man was left floundering in the water from which he was hauled by someone nearby throwing him a rope from the pier. Where was 'Candid Camera'? What a shot it would have been!.

Another fact is that many of these people go out without even the most basic gear to help them out of trouble. They have neither oars nor a suitable anchor plus rope long enough to reach the bottom. One such I was talking to on the beach in the harbour had just launched his 14 foot plywood boat. Noticing that he had a rather elderly outboard motor, I asked what he had as alternative propulsion should the engine fail. 'Oh', says he, 'I'm OK', dived into a locker in the stern and produced two plywood PING-PONG BATS! - as oars. 'As for moving a boat, a pair of teaspoons would do as well and you could carry them in your pocket', I said. On being asked about an anchor he produced a railway fishplate and 12 or 15 feet of clothes line - ideal for the village pond!. A very few will ask us if conditions are suitable to go out. If told no, they do not always believe us. If the water inside the harbour is fairly calm and the sun shining, what can go wrong? And away they go to discover for themselves.............

On all of the long coastline of Northumberland our patch is the worst for tides. We stand out on a blunt headland, the land trending inwards north and south of us. The Farne Islands, lying athwart the main tidal streams split and divide the flood and ebb into strong channels. Depending on the strength and direction of the wind these can cause serious problems to even large boats at times. Anybody who has crossed the 'Fairway', the inner sound, in a flood tide and a S to SE wind will know what I mean.

In spite of all the valuable advice printed in the Yachting papers on safety precautions, there are still far too many who take a chance, knowing that they and their outfit are inadequate but relying on the Lifeboat and other rescue services to come to their aid. To these people I say, 'don't be so selfish, remember that your stupidity puts others at risk forbye yourselves'. If I had my way, they would be charged the expense incurred by their rescue, perhaps making them think twice if not more.

Now to get on to a more pleasant task. Those who start off in a rowing or sailing boat learn more in a week than the power boat men learn in 10 years. To anyone daft enough to learn the ways of the sea I say, 'try to get an experienced person at first; you can't become a sailor by reading about it in a book as it takes practical training'. Always ask advice from locals, they know their patch. Generally a polite question will produce a wealth of information that will stand you in good stead. A sailing boat is a different kettle of fish from a mechanically driven one. They have a feeling of life about them, they are driven by a natural force and are susceptible to that force because it is not a constant thing like an engine beating out its regular revolutions. Every little variation of the wind is felt by the sails and transmitted to the fabric of the boat. The wind is pulling the boat along all the time and minute alterations effect the trim. To the person handling the helm and sails it can be like playing a musical instrument, needing delicate adjustments all the time to make a harmonious whole. Instead of battering on in a line from A to B, a sail boat depends on the vagaries of the wind. There is a constant need for careful calculation. It can be the angle of the sails, either with or adverse; of the tide; an awareness all the time, every little puff making the boat twitch – not a good simile –but the best I can do to describe the feeling of life it brings. Starting off in a sailer you get lessons never to be forgotten.

That is why the old generations, brought up in sail, took such pride in their boats. In a book I read about small sailing craft some years ago the writer advocated the superiority of pleasure craft over fishing boats, dismissing the latter as 'poor boats, built for poor men'. Maybe he thought that a bit of varnished mahogany and chromium plate was the height of marine elegance. There has never been a yacht yet to better the performance or sea keeping qualities of a fishing boat.

Herreshoff, the famous American yacht designer at the turn of the century, was a guest of a Tyneside business man. A lot of wealthy men on the Tyne used to own cobles or mules(sharp–sterned cobles) at that time. They had them built for the pleasure of racing them using crews of local fishermen. As a small boy I recall seeing one here, lying behind the houses down from the Dolphin Cafe. She was unusual in being carvel (smooth planks) instead of clench built (overlap planks), but still a coble.

How she got there, or what she was used for, I know not. I was told that she had been raced at Blyth against conventional yachts and had beaten them hands down so many times that she was handicapped severely to take all the sport out of owning her. The man who was host to Herreshoff asked him to examine a racing coble to see if he could suggest any improvements. Having gone over the boat, the usual broad plank build, he said that had it been built carvel style it may have helped, otherwise he could not fault the design. The coble was the result and it is history that the first life saving boat on this coast was a Northumbrian coble fitted with air boxes and stationed at the Mill Burn at Bamburgh.

It is time to return to the annals of the village and how we lived 70 odd years ago. And to write of the people who lived during the depression years when men were desperate for work, any work, and of the men who manned those boats I have mentioned before, slyly injecting the Norse connection when I can. Life in a village where every face was as well known as your own could be far from idyllic at times. 'Aabody kens aabody!'. If you sneezed on Monday morning going to school, somebody would tell your mother before teatime. It was like living in a box with a glass lid. Little went on that was not public knowledge soon. There was no 'wireless', some had the old horn gramophones belting out Harry Lauder and other popular stars of the day in the squeaky voices created by the record spinning above its recommended rate.

My memory is good enough that I can mind my father leaving the cottage, seeing him going away, food wrapped in brown paper under his arm, down to the harbour, away to the nights herring fishing. We lived in Mayfield Row then, locally called Sandy Raa. We had shifted from the house at the harbour where I was born as the Mayfield one had a garden and my mother could dry the washing in better conditions. It also had an outside washhouse, handy for my father to make or repair his gear. That would be in 1914. Houses on the Bank 'Hied' were occupied by Coastguards and I remember going with father went he went there to volunteer for the Navy. The war years were hard on our community, food being scarce. Flour was a mixture of all sorts of seeds, bread from it was grey. At one time sugar could not be had for love nor money. Treacle was tried to sweeten tea, but it turned it grey, so you were eating grey bread and dripping and drinking grey tea. The papers came by train and I mind seeing photos of the trenches. Various army personnel and materials passed through. My mother found it hard to make ends meet, the few shillings from my father's allowance was not enough to feed us. She started to bait a line for my cousin, Dan, a laddie of 15 who, with another of the same age, 'Little Bill' Robson, went with my two older uncles who were at first too old for service. The larger boats had been laid up or sold as there were no men to crew them, so the remaining fishermen carried on with the sailing cobles. My grandfather, although elderly, kept going with two other old men in his coble 'Britain's Pride'. The other boat owned by my mother's clan was the 'Selina'. Mother got 10/- (50p) a week for baiting Dan's line. I recall once when we had nothing in the house to eat except bread and OXO, a beef extract still available today. My mother had to sell some of my father's gear to get a bit extra cash. Finally it was over, with the inevitable changes, but the tenor of the fishermen remained unchanged apart from no longer pursuing the herring.

To start long lining in winter a typical fishing family's day was thus: If the weather was suitable, an early start was made, any time from 3 am onwards by the man. Ours being a tidal harbour, were the boats not moved down into the deeper areas, it would affect the whole days programme. Should a boat be too late or be grounded, several hours would elapse before the tide came in again and by then it would be too late. The fish train left at 4.15 pm and that was when the catch had to be landed, boxed and transported to the station. His wife would have to be on the go by 5 am.

So the day could be something like this, perhaps the time of year December on a fine quiet morning. The husband gets up at 4am, lights a candle, and gives the fire a rake to clear it of ashes and small cinders. If any red coals are left overnight, he sets the kettle on, surrounds it with sticks to boil up quickly, and gets the teapot ready. Then he has a couple of slices of home baked bread and butter, strong sweet tea and a dash of milk. All this can take only 15 or 20 minutes and he is out into the quiet dark of the morning. A pause to scan the sky and assess the 'feel' of the atmosphere. He is fully clothed and sea booted, wearing a short oilskin coat over his 'barkit slowp' −a strong cotton overall without buttons, tanned brown in the net preservative − and worn over his home knitted 'gansey' of

44

blue wool. The 'slowp' reaches from his neck to his waist, saving his gansey from wear and dirt, and keeping out the wind.

His short oilskin breeks and sou-wester are rolled around a slice or two of bread and butter and placed in the end of the oval basket, the 'Swull'. It holds his baited line which stands on a flat base of planks on four legs about shoulder high. These were a feature of all line fishermen's homes, either at the house end or beside the garden wall. The line-stand, as it was termed, enabled him to get the line easily on to his back. It had to be carefully handled so as not to disturb the rows of baited hooks in the low end or 'swull' mouth. The line-stand also did duty as cover for two large pails of mussels and a medium sized one of limpets to bait the line ashore. The line was in three parts usually, two parts equalling one complete line taken to sea, one part left behind from the previous days fishing unbaited so the baiter had something to get on with. When the fisherman returned, half the returned line was attached to the (hopefully) ready baited piece and baited up, the last piece unbent and left for the next day.

And so as he proceeds down through the quiet houses, now with lights glimmering through the blinds as the fishing community stirs itself for another days toil. Arriving at the harbour and making for where his boat is moored —more by instinct than anything else, for there were no lights on the piers then – some of the other men, down already, help him to lower his 'swull' on to the ground as the crew, usually four in number, assemble and get their eyes used to the dark. At that time in the morning it is too dim to see. The lines are lowered carefully down into the boat, one of the crew having gone in to receive them, and the last few words spoken to the men around:-

'Aye, its fine the now, but we cud git a bit feyne breeze wi the flud afore th'days oot. Probably bey frae th' s'th east wi that bit white frost' or

'Wer ganna gie th' back pairt o' Farengroonds a go this mornin, owld Wull wis shot doon wi' ees north end yisterday, an gat a few gud haddocks ont'.

And one by one the boats crept out and down towards the harbour entrance. Two men at the great 16 foot sweeps, another setting

45

the mast ready, the skipper grunting with the effort of lying over the 'skud' shipping the long rudder, the soft crash as the pintles met the gudgeon, the clack as the long curved tiller is slotted over the rudder head.

Cobles carried a short and a long mast. Normally the long mast was used but, if it came on to blow, the short was set, the spare one being used as a bowsprit. The rig was simplicity itself, lending itself to swift handling. The jib tack cringle would be bent on the bowsprit end and shoved outboards through the gammon, the single rope halliard fast to the peak cringle ready for hoisting, the sheet laid handy to the foot of the mast. The mainsail, a dipping lug laid along what would be the lee side, with the half ring in the yard hooked into the 'traveller'. There was a single block halliard tied loosely on the weather belaying pin, with the tack cringle hooked to the gun tackle down-haul on the weather shoulder and all was set.

FEAR NOT, DEAR READER, at this point, ALL WILL BE MADE PLAIN LATER, as these strange sounding terms are explained!.

So, with the boat clearing the harbour mouth and the skipper feeling the 'bit air o'wund' on his cheek, he would get on to the weather quarter, pick up the sheet from where it came through the 'dead-eye' or 'numb block' while the rest of the crew got the sail up and mast headed. The downhaul of the halliard was passed under the pin under the gunnel and 'bighted' fast, the tack downhaul hauled home and belayed, the jib hauled up, the main sheet adjusted over the skipper's knee with one hand while he steered with the other. And off the boat went, sliding through the water with barely a whisper.

Leaving our mariners to proceed, we return to the cottage where the family is sleeping, the wife stretching out the short time left in her warm bed before rising at 5 am. At least the room is warm, for the room in most of houses is living room, kitchen, bedroom and workroom. The fire, banked up with coal before her husband left, burns brightly, the big cast iron kettle steaming gently on the hob at the side of the grate and the lid clicking as it lifts a little to ease out a puff of steam. The two bairns aged say, 6 and 8, are still sleeping contentedly. The last moment arrives and so she climbs out of bed, crosses to the table in front of the window and puts a match to the circle burner paraffin lamp of polished brass.

Local boats in Seahouses Harbour - 1905/1910.

Soon a warm yellow glow lightens the room as she dresses and has a cup of tea. All this is done quickly without any wasted movement. The husband's cup and saucer, knife and spoon, are put into an enamel dish to one side. The heavy curtains are opened, the glass of the window obscured by a dark blue linen roller blind. The lamp is then carefully placed on the window sill, adjusted to the best height by short pieces of flat plank. A piece of old sail is placed over the oilcloth table cover and the 'swull' with the tangled portion of yesterdays line is brought in, the empty 'swull' to receive the new baited line. Next she rolls up the 'clooty' mats off the centre of the floor, exposing the linoleum, and, covering the space with another piece of old sail, places a square wooden stool or backless chair on the floor, in front of which was placed a small wooden tub. Then she brought in the two pails of mussels and one pail of limpets gathered the previous day.

The mussels were always covered with fresh water but the limpets

47

Seahouses and Harbour, Northumberland

Local and Scottish boats c.1910. In the centre, a Zulu.

were left dry. There would be ice on the mussel pails and she might have to pour a little hot water from the kettle to thaw it. If the frost had been severe, the husband would bring them indoors before going to the harbour. Donning an oilskin apron, she would sit down with the first pail between her and the fire, an old enamel pie dish between her knees, and a tin bath at her side to receive the empty shells. A half dozen mussels would be put into the pie dish and 'skyenning' would begin, using a ground down table knife with about two iches of blade, leaf shaped and sharpened on both sides. Taking the mussel in the palm of one hand, with the flat base out-wards, she would insert the point of the knife between the two halves of the shell and with a quick, dexterous flip, turn the knife around the inside, cutting the great muscle that closed it. With a scooping motion out would come the meat to fall with a plop into the tub at her feet. The whole operation was over in seconds, the process repeated until all the mussels were shelled.

Meantime the clock ticking on arrives at 6 am. Mother leaves her stool for a wee while to waken her eldest who, bleary eyed, slurps a cup of sweet tea and prepares to help by shelling as many of the limpets as he can. It is much easier to do, using an old tea spoon. He gets out his stool, dons an old apron and puts his little wooden tub for the limpets at his toes. He grips the first limpet inside his thumb and forefinger, runs the spoon around the body of the limpet and out it pops. Although not a lot of skill is needed, it is a sore affair, as I can tell you!. The thumb and finger gripping hard on the sharp shell, sometimes serrated like a saw, soon nicks and chafes the skin until blood comes. So he labours on, brought in at an early age, helping adults who, in their time, had to do the same thing. By 8.30 am the bairns are washed and breakfasted on bread, butter, boiled egg, tea and off to school. They return after 12 noon, leaving at 12.40 pm for afternoon school, and home for tea at 3.45 pm.

Meanwhile the work flows on, the wife, having stood at the table untangling the line, cleaning off the bits of weed, old bait and starfish off it, then re-baiting and relaying the line anew. She worked from left to right, each hook was baited with the mussel first, held by its 'tongue', a tough black proturberance out of the soft body, the rest around the hook, the point somewhere in its 'whiskers', the fine threads that held it in its shell. A small mussel was backed by a limpet, alternatives being done by baiting some hooks with limpets only. They were tougher than mussels but not so well taken by the fish.

All this time she was keeping an eye on the pans simmering on the hob, having taken a bit of time to prepare the simple main meal of the day. Often it was Scotch broth, made in a big cast iron pan, with vegetables and a big knuckle bone from the butchers. Some days, if she had time, there would be a suet dumpling steamed in a basin. To follow, a rice pudding or a boiled suet raisin dumpling –a 'clootie'. Food was plain but nourishing and cheap. Apart from the rationing of the war years nobody went hungry –there was always fish!. Supper might be boiled or roasted salt herring and tatties in their jackets. Everybody had their 'kit' of herring salted down, as they said, 'winter beef'. If conditions at sea were kind, the man would be home by 1 or 2 o'clock.

After the meal, should the tide suit, he might get the two mussel pails up for the next day or go and get the limpets, returning to

Seahouses Harbour c.1908, all sail boats.

'redd' ,i.e clear the line, for his wife who by now was on the
second part of the newly landed line. It was often about 6 pm
before all was finished. Then the wife washed the floor, got the
supper ready and, likely as not, started knitting. If the tide had not
been suitable for the husband's help with bait−gathering she had to
do it herself, often walking over a mile to get enough limpets to
fill her pail, then come back to her work at home. How they
managed to do without a 48 hour day, I'll never know!.
It was impossible to go through winter without bad weather. There
were days and weeks when the onshore winds brought heavy seas
crashing over the harbour walls. The time, however, was not spent
in idleness − no fear!.
The women took the opportunity to clean, bake, wash and knit. The
men repaired and made new crabbing gear, knitting the nets by hand
for to cover the 'creaves'(crab and lobster pots).   The bent ribs
holding the net cover had to be sought in the hedgerows, maybe

needing 4 or 5 mile walks into the country. Ash was mainly used but also elm, willow and hazel. Nothing was discarded until it was absolutely beyond redemption. Old lines were used to lash the stones that sank the creaves and to lash on the net covers. Old rope was used to make the bridles that attached them to the main tow. Driftwood was gathered on the shore, suitable pieces used to make the creave bottoms. What a lesson in thrift for todays throwaway society!. Idleness was a cardinal sin and to be called 'lazy' was one of the worst things you could be accused of!. They took work, and I mean work in all that word entails, with a gusto that cannot be described. They toiled with mighty hearts, often for a bare living. They had to accept money for their labours, unable to better the system of selling through a series of middlemen. Manys the time in telling folk this they have said, 'why didn't you sell your own stuff? without realising that a man could only do one job at a time. He couldn't be a fisherman and retailer at the same time. The time factor and distances involved were beyond him

Out of the poor returns they had to find enough to maintain their most valuable possessions, their boats, on which they depended, not only for a living, but for their very lives. Their gear had to be of good quality, too, but they never grumbled about the money they had to spend to maintain it. It was essential for survival, always must it come first. They knew the value of money as they got so little that 'every penny was a prisoner' but they were not mean, meanness being also a cardinal sin. Their wants were simple, and despite the harshness of their lives, they were usually contented with their lot. They did not wear their hearts on their sleeves and to show emotion was embarrassing. A lad seen with his arm round his girl's waist was dismissed as a 'fond fool'.

Some readers may be tempted to wonder why life like this was accepted and why do I not condemn it. To them I say that it was the way of its time, no different from long hours in cotton mills.

But to return to those times. There was no physical cruelty but the spoken word could be as cutting. Children were well cared for but kept in their place. 'Look at everything but touch nothing', we were often admonished. Elders had to be, and were, respected, swearing was frowned upon but, of course, there were always the few who brought out the odd 'strong word'. Neither was there any filthy talk, four letter words, other obscenities or blaspheming. They were all subject to human temptations; the odd bairn was born out of

51

Harbour from the Magazine c.1905. At the middle pier is the paddle tug for towing in and out in calm weather.

wedlock, but at the same time they were surprisingly moral. It seems the Norsemen had a similar outlook as a pair of bodies found in a peat bog in Denmark and dating back nearly 2000 years, were of a couple found in adultery, beaten to death and thrown into the bog with the wooden staves used for their execution. Again, I make no apology. Yes, times were hard – but we lacked the 'loads of money' syndrome and the crime and vandalism – and we could play out in safety. There are those who wish that were possible today.

During the 1939–45 war fishing by trawler was at a standstill with the vessels armed and converted to war duties. A few small boats operated close to the coasts, so the fish proliferated into enormous shoals. In the years immediately after 1945 there was a great up-surge in the industry. Boats were in great demand as the returning fishermen wanted to resume their calling as soon as possible. But an ambiguous situation existed regarding the distribution and marketing of the fish. Buyers bought at a supposedly fixed price, as did the middlemen, and the retailer and the consumer in the fish shop, prices being determined by a government body. The problem for the fishermen was that while the buyers, etc., were working on fixed and guaranteed prices dependent only on the availability of supply, the price got by fishermen could fluctuate – up to the fixed price – but down as low as possible. It was not a *fixed* price for the fishermen, but a *ceiling* price, grossly unfair to men who needed money to buy new boats and gear. I myself was landing prime large whiting, the control price fixed at 3/8p per stone, but getting only 1/6p on the market i.e. less than half price. Our earnings were only half of what they should have been, somebody else was making a killing! The same happened with shellfish, the crab trade, which the smaller boats depended on to make up their earnings when fish were scarce. Steady but unspectacular wages could be made at it, the price being 7/– per stone, a stone of crabs averaging 10 crabs. The Government of the day purchased 14,000 cases of canned Russian crab. When they were distributed round the shops, the price of fresh crab fell by exactly half to 3/6p per stone. Meantime the price of gear was going up by leaps and bounds. Seine net rope which I bought in 1946 for £4.00 per cwt for sisal, a rope inferior to manila rope but all we could get at the time, had risen to £16.00 per cwt in 1948.

Herring fishing resumed, west coast boats fit out for ring netting, Firth of Forth boats fished alongside local boats on the local grounds, and for a while the old days were back. Came the purse nets and the herring went. Meantime the seine net was abandoned and the otter trawl commenced.

The Icelanders had finally put paid to their grounds being fished by the British. The large trawler fleets vanished, smaller boats were scraping over the bottom of the North Sea and the result of over–fishing was smaller catches. Lads left the fishing for shore jobs, the local fleet started to thin out and the older men retired.

With a handful of big boats barely holding on, a few small ones with minimum crews shell fishing, a small fleet of passenger boats working like mad in the short season taking people to the Farne Islands, the local boatbuilders yard started after the war with no orders for new boats – a bleak outlook.

The EEC has not made life easy for the fishermen who are subject to pressure unknown to their fathers. Directives come which we, at times, see as irrelevant, neither do we feel that people from our own Ministries are totally supportive. For instance:– a net cannot discriminate between species of fish. Suppose, as has happened, that catches of haddock are to be restricted to conserve stocks. The fisherman who catches cod and haddock in the same net – because they happen to be swimming together – is forced to throw the dead haddocks overboard. If they aren't being landed, they must be being conserved. What the eye doesn't see......! Nets are condemned for having too small a mesh and may be scrapped at, literally, a moments notice. Other EEC countries are boosting their mens' claims at the expense of ours. That is not just a 'Seahouses' view, ask the men of Newlyn!

A fatal weakness on the part of fishermen was that their spirit of independence worked against them. They were incapable in the main of organising themselves unless it was against their own kind. I have already said that when a new method of fishing was tried and found to be successful, those who could not, or would not, try it wanted it stopped. In the last century it was found that a certain rig up of a hand line was able to catch cod and haddock in the late spring and summer by jigging bare hooks on a sinker close to the bottom. Previously you used a baited hook, a slow, tedious process. The Seahouses men operating the new rig were able to land good catches. Other villages, using the old method, were jealous of its success so they agitated to have it banned as being cruel to fish! I could never see the difference between catching a fish by a baited hook or a bare one. In time they took to the new method!

A more recent annoyance over the last 20 years or so is the growth of scuba diving. No doubt the majority who practice it are decent, law–abiding people. Regrettably a few seem to be there for what they can take by way of shellfish. At first no fishermen minded them taking a crab or lobster for their own use but it was too much when they started to rob the creaves on the sea bottom. Having had mine opened and the contents taken down to the very bait itself, the creave was left unable to catch anything.

I know that they had been opened as the door–lacing knot was not my tieing and the last creave was left open. Another so–called 'joke' was to cut a man's tow and re–tie it foul of a wreck so he could not haul his creaves in. That was found when two lads who were real divers and were salvaging were asked if they could free

The Outer Harbour at low tide. Two schooners lie in the Inner Harbour. 1910.

it. I've even had a diver surface beside the propellor, fortunately for him it was out of gear at the time.

Now a fisherman is subject to certain legal requirements before he can operate. His catch is subject to inspection by a Fisheries Officer at any time and must comply with certain measurements for shell and for round fish. These skin divers are seldom asked to show what they have got. One was boiling shellfish and selling them at one of the caravan sites. I found a carrier bag full of lobster shells below that site, noting the remains of five lobsters, three of which were undersized. A fisherman caught with only one such would be fined heavily.

Some years ago a diver was drowned at Howick rocks. When his body was found, he was clutching a plastic bag containing lobsters. I cannot guess how many times, and at what cost, the rescue services have been called out to their aid. Several have been saved by pure luck.   The hard thing is that these people all have expensive equipment which in turn means well-paid jobs.   Do they not realise they are taking a man's living by theft – and expecting the self same men to come to their rescue when they are in trouble.

Thankfully not all are alike and I am sorry for the decent ones as they have to suffer for the hooligan minority.   It must be said that wherever they have been there has been friction with the local fishermen.   The men who operate the passenger boats to the Farne Islands have had problems, too, trying to avoid divers surfacing close to their boats when under way.   A plan of operational areas for divers is on display at the Harbour Office, but still they crop up in unexpected places.   Certainly the divers are well organised as when any attempt has been made to control their activities they have been able to call on powerful allies to defend them. It is all tied in with the great Mogul of today – Sport.

I am fortunate that I lived through a time, hard though it was, but having a measure of freedom about it – when to go to sea and pit your wits against it – to strive, but also to live without the necessity to fill in reams of paper when you came ashore.   When your boat was something to be proud of, and you could belong to a society of men of the sea who went about their daily work quietly and without fuss.   Yes, I consider myself lucky!.

5.   THE HARBOUR.

While there has been a landing place for boats for centuries, it was the lime trade that gave impetus to the construction of a proper harbour, followed in later years by the rise in importance of the herring fishing.   In the early days before the quarrying of stone to build the harbour began, the harbour area would have presented a much different appearance.   The stone came from the immediate vicinity of the harbour and the drift holes bored to split the rock can still be found.   The method was to bore a two inch diameter hole deep into the rock mass, pack it with new burnt lime, top up with water and plug the hole with clay.   The lime expanded under the action of the water and the pressure split the rock.   Removing large masses of stone caused the cliff to erode in places so we cannot estimate how much was lost.   Stone was also used to build the older houses in the harbour area.   The recess in the cliff line below the Seafield Filling Station was an old quarry and where the spring issues from the rock at the south end was used for 'barking' herring nets.   Brick furnaces for heating the large iron vats are still visible. The quarry was used to house the cobles and mules in the herring fishing season, to relieve space in the harbour, only a few old men keeping their boats moored on the beach south of the slipway.

The original harbour is now the inner one and today's pier was the outer one.   It was much higher then, with a massive sea wall culminating in a club like end with a beacon lantern on a wooden frame, the 'low' light.   The 'high' light was a lantern in brackets at the gable end of the house at the top of the Malley Stairs, the steps leading up to the 'Nick', the lane behind the Old Ship Hotel, which runs along to the 'Black Swan' and 'Schooner' Inns.   The two lights brought into line were the leading marks for entering the harbour. By day two pole beacons served the same purpose.   There was not enough room on the surface of the old outer pier for a cart, just a footpath.   Opposite the short pier end a piece projected leaving just enough room for a small coasting vessel to enter.   As there was no outer breakwater they had, during heavy seas, to shut the harbour mouth with large square wooden beams dropped down a slot in the pier ends.   A small crane situated on the arm opposite to the short pier end did this.   On the inside of the outer arm the main pier sloped down from a narrow path inside the sea wall to the harbour bottom, so no craft was able to berth against it.   Loading facilities were from the short pier end, in and along the kilns, and the head of the harbour opposite the kilns.   The latter projected on the north end past the pier on to a beach, the pier at this point being only about eight feet in breadth.   Where the lifeboat house now stands was a cart access up the bank past the kilns. On the edge of the shore stood a primitive latrine, open to the sky.

The harbour belonged to the Lord Crewe Trustees, who administered the trust set up by Lord Crewe, who had owned Bamburgh Castle and its dependencies.   He willed that various charities be set up, including gear for refloating stranded ships, the firing of a cannon during foggy weather, a girls' school and others.   An anchor and chains for salvage work may still be seen at Bamburgh Castle Keep.

After the collapse of the lime trade, luckily there was an upsurge in the herring trade.   By the late 1870s it was realised that the harbour as it was could not accomodate the number of boats using it. Not only was it too small but coasting ships were arriving with supplies for the trade and it was a tight squeeze, to say the least. The Trustees decided to fund the harbour extension, work starting on 2nd March 1886.   That coincided with the arrival of my Aunt Isabella, who lived to be a hundred and three years old.

The outer harbour required the removal of a rock which had been a hazard to the approach to the harbour. It was demolished and the broken stone incorporated into the new pier. Landing facilities were increased enormously and, as I said earlier in the book, over 300 boats discharged herring at the height of the season. In spite of the addition of the outer breakwater the 'New' harbour was no use if there was any sea on. There was a nasty 'run' and boats could not be kept in it, only the original harbour was safe. It could only be used for discharging and boats had to 'weekend' at Holy Island or Beadnell unless the weather was very fine. The quality of the building material was poor and it was not long before it was crumbling in places. The long pier end had to be repaired about the start of the 1914 war. I remember seeing the diver working, filling in a large hole at bottom level. I used to be terrified of his suit hanging up to dry.   There must have been a serious defect as in later years the whole pier end subsided slightly. That is why the lighthouse is out of plumb. In recent years a complete cement casing has been built around the end to protect it.

In the early 1930s cracks started to appear in the centre of the breakwater finally turning into a hole halfway down the structure. Every gale contributed its quota of destruction until the whole centre was down and open to the breakers. Rebuilding began in the middle 1930s but with a difference. Massive pre-cast concrete blocks were built up, layer by layer, and the new breakwater was length-ened considerably. Where it had had a dog-leg in it, it was made straight. The design was asked for by the local fishermen and was a great improvement over the former design, not only because the harbour mouth was actually wider, but there was less 'run' coming into the harbour. In heavy seas the old breakwater caused a strong current to sweep across the harbour mouth, shoving a vessel entering to leeward on to the long pier end. There is still a current but with the breakwater end more to seaward there is more room to manoeuvre.

Had the Farne Islands not been where they are it would have been almost impossible to have a harbour either here or at Holy Island. The harbour here is fully exposed to the north, but as the Islands stretch nearly three miles across, running roughly WNW to ESE, they break the force of a northerly gale. At Holy Island, it works in reverse. The islands stretch across the east and south-east approaches, stopping the easterly gales with their heavy seas from going into the anchorage. The effect may be seen here in a severe northerly gale for, while it is bad enough about the harbour, it is much heavier at Beadnell and further south. Holy Island itself breaks the northerlies and at Seahouses the 'Rock ends' break the easterlies.

Many visitors wonder what the little round topped stone building was for. It was built for storage of explosives for the 1886 extension and used again for the 1930s rebuilding. The rocks around this 'magazine' are honeycombed with caves and natural fissures. The opening through the rocks below the building itself is called the 'Rummle Kirn' or 'Rumble Chum'. The caves were called the 'Smuggling Holes' and it is quite possible they were used for that purpose. Every nook and cranny along the shore both north and south of the harbour had its name, used, and handed down for generations.

Entering the harbour, two white painted posts marked the rocks on the south side of the 'haven'. During the 1930s roadstone was shipped to the Tyne by tug and lighters. A lighter broke adrift in a heavy sea, collided with the innermost post and broke it. The outer survived until recent years when age and sea worms caused its down fall as well. Where the pleasure boats are moored in summer is known as the 'Flukehole' because before it was deepened it had a large shallow sandy pool at low water with a lot of immature flatfish ('flukes') in it. It was also our summer playground when we were young.

We learnt to handle an oar at an early age helping the men who ferried the herring from the drifters at anchor in the 'Roads' outside the harbour mouth when they had missed the tide and could not get in. The ferrying was done in small flat-bottomed 'skiffs', 16 to 18 feet long, about 6 feet beam and operated by one man. They tied up alongside the drifter and the herrings in boxes were slung aboard the skiff by derrick until it was down to about 6 inches freeboard. The bow was upturned to allow the oars a bit extra height and the boat was rowed into the shallow water in the harbour alongside the horse and cart which took the load up to the herring yard. There was only one motor lorry then. It could only operate off the quays.

Cornish Luggers from St.Ives c.1905.

It couldn't go down where the horses went!. After the cart was loaded the horse had to make a flying start to get up the beach on to the slip and then to the road. The carter would yell and crack his whip, the horse lunging and going at a gallop, clods of wet sand flying behind its hooves. It would slow down gradually as it reached the drier sand, the hooves scrabbling madly as it got to the slip, which was paved with smooth oblong limestone blocks. On the level it was an easy pull for a few yards until reaching the bottom of the steep bank, then it was nearly on tip-toes until at the top.

At times the harbour used to dry out almost to the entrance and we explored every square foot of it, turning over the stones for green crabs and small eels. When the tide came in we sat on the old pier end and fished for 'podlies' as we called the young coalfish that swarmed into the harbour after dead herring lost off the drifters. There were also common flounders we called 'blackbacks' which we caught with a hook on the bottom of the line. Sometimes they were as big as a good-sized dinner plate. Any sizeable fish were given to the lobstermen to bait their creaves. A favourite place at almost high water was from the rocks to the south of the harbour area known as the 'Britsen Hole'. Here a pipe from the herring yards discharged its murky water full of bits of herring liver, etc. Quite large podlies of well over a pound were caught there. The remains of the old pipes are still there but nothing flows through them now and the podlies no longer swim there.

We all had our model sailing herring boats made by some of the men who were noted for the replicas they made, with little more than a clasp knife. They were hollowed out and decked over, with a lead keel and the two-masted keelboat lugger rig and sail. They sailed exceedingly well because they were well made and many a race was held across the 'Flukehole'. We also used a water pool we called the 'Big Hole'. As it only filled at high tide it was useable most of the time. When there was a strong westerly wind, we could get a good voyage for our boats from the sand at the slip to the rocks. We made a special boat for this, from a barrel stave with a piece of iron barrel hoop for a keel, a short mast and square brown paper sail well aft. They really used to shift, scooting over the water in the gusts of wind – great fun!.

It wasn't all fun and games, however, for the harbour was often the scene of high drama especially in winter. Being a tidal harbour it needed a certain amount of water for the boats to enter. If there happened to be a swell on the shore, as there was often, it was hazardous or downright dangerous because of the shallow approach. Once committed the boat had to come on until it was safely inside. The advent of engines took away a lot of the risk that sailing boats were subject to. A red flag flying on the end of the pier mast was the signal for danger; a red flag over a blue meant enough water to enter, but hazardous. If conditions were very bad a truss of straw was burnt as flames and smoke were visible further out to sea.

There were always a few old hands on the look-out those days, to keep a watch for mishaps. The dreaded double bangs of the maroon alerted all the village, the signal that the lifeboat was needed The old lifeboat house, the one for the old pulling and sailing boat, stood where the Dolphin Cafe is now. The lifeboat was pulled out of the house and taken down the bank by the side of where the new life-boat house stands. She also had to be pulled up it again after each service. With all or nearly all the able bodied men at sea, it was a real job the launchers faced. Many a time I've seen a score or more of women and lassies tailing on the launching cables. Once afloat the best situation was just under the lee of the breakwater end where it was the practice to dash out in case of a boat in trouble, because any accident was most liable to occur near the harbour mouth. A lot of land folk could not understand this at all, they thought the lifeboat should be outside among the boats, but a moment of reflection will show that it was easier to row out into the sea than run in before the seas to pick up survivors. A heavy lifeboat running on a sea could land on top of men in the water. There was never a shortage of volunteers for a scratch crew, sometimes including farm hands and tradesmen.

With the influx of new folks from other places in latter years, the sound of the maroons brought them down with their cars, causing a lot of obstruction to the launching. They were determined not to miss anything. The fact that boats and lives were in danger was only secondary to them, it seems. They wanted the thrill and excitement of something they had never seen before without considering the difficulty they made for those trying to do the work. On one day there was a very nasty sea, and in the dark, a Scottish boat was running for the harbour. I was hurrying along to the pier end when a car passed me, ran right up to the railings around the end and put his full headlamps on to the windows of the boat's wheelhouse as she was almost level with the breakwater end. The man steering the boat would be completely blinded. Fortunately somebody at the railing banged on the car roof to make the idiot switch his lights off. He had put that boat and crew in danger. Today the lifeboat is called out by radio doing away with the maroons. It makes me smile when I hear people talking about how lifeboats can go through any sort of sea conditions. Of course they can, they are specially built to do so! But the humans who form the crew are only flesh and blood and can only endure so much. When a lifeboat has capsized, the boat has always been recovered, but not the crew. A few weeks after I was born, a small ketch with a cargo of rock salt was wrecked inside the harbour on the rocks south of the 'hammer head', the short arm projecting south from the outer pier end. It was blowing a whole gale and more from the NNW. The lifeboat was payed down to the wreck on a hawser from the middle pier end. The wind was so strong that the oars were useless, blowing about

By the 1930s, all were motor boats. These are from Eyemouth or the Firth of Forth.

like straws. When the ketch filled with water it melted the cargo of salt and as she was badly damaged she was broken up.

I remember a small coasting steamer grounded in the harbour mouth. She had broken her tail shaft just inside the stern-tube, losing the propellor and shaft stub. The water gushed in through the tube and the engineer and crew struggled to plug it without success. As this happened, by lucky chance, the local boats towed her into the shore where she took the ground inside the pier end. I cannot remember now if she was plugged and towed away or if a new shaft was fitted, its so long ago. It would take another book to record the stories of storm, shipwreck and other incidents over my lifetime!.

6.   STRANGER THAN FICTION............

in which I am going have a niggle about some of the inaccuracies I have come across in picture and print.

The Victorians were hopelessly romantic in the ways they depicted sailors and the sea. In their paintings and photographs fishermen were usually in suitably posed situations. It could be a highly scenic setting, or at sea in impossible waves, sailing at impossible angles with impossibly set sails. If ashore it showed, invariably, a group of seabooted, bearded worthies in 'ganseys' and 'sou'westers'. The idea was to convey to the layman the essential affinity of the subject with the sea and things maritime. In the same way, the countryman appeared in a long smock, chewing a piece of straw! Recently I saw a photo of two elderly fishermen, posed outside a cottage door, one seated, one standing. Both were wearing 'sou'westers', their obviously Sunday 'ganseys' and polished boots, not sea boots, and with large grins peeking through tidily combed beards. Fishermen never looked like this!

Over recent decades various books have appeared about fishing and fishing boats. Some are very well illustrated with old photos of the fishing harbours of yesteryear. Regrettably, homework seems not always to have been done so that the captions can be misleading. In one picture, two boats were putting out to sea captioned 'Zulu and Scaffie'. One was a keelboat, or fifie if you like, the other was a Cornish lugger. Another, a postcard entitled the 'Cobles of Craster', could only offer 3 or 4 plastic dinghies on it.

Somewhere it was suggested that, in the harbours which had water as opposed to beaches, the 'mules', i.e sharp-ended cobles, were preferred while the flat-sterned cobles were more liable to damage. In my experience many fishermen had two boats, a coble and a mule. The mule was used for line fishing and was a bit better than the coble for running before the sea. The coble, with the more roomy stern, was preferred for shell fishing, but they could be used for the same purpose if required. The weak point of a coble was that, with the sea coming up astern, they had to be nursed a bit, as the deep forefront used to grip the water, only counterbalanced by the long rudder. They had to present the boat's quarter to the sea whereas the mule's sharp stern would sink in a bit and give a grip. To give an idea of how it worked, slide a plastic dish down something slippery. It will probably either turn round or move out of a straight line. Now shove the point of a tack through one side of the bottom and that tack will guide it in a straight line.

'Huh', you say, 'what are you all steamed up about, nobody knows any better!'. That isn't my point. If any of those shiney tin

Another 1930s shot. This one is a motor herring keelboat. It could be the 'Supreme' from Fisherrow.

pollution wagons cluttering our roads were referred to as 'Barras', wouldn't there be an outcry!. 'What, call the sacred motor car a barra!'. Think about it!

A couple of decades or so ago, it was decided that the seal population on the Farne Islands was reaching dangerous proportions, both for their own healths' sake and for the effect it was having on the fishing. The decision was taken to thin them out, 'cull', was the term. It was to be done as humanely as possible.

Norwegian hunters would do the necessary and remove the carcases. What a tizzy that caused!. The 'Anties' were screaming, 'save the seals'. No doubt some people were genuinely interested but this sort of thing brings the long-hairs and weirdies.

The village was inundated with scores of people, TV men and the ever-present newspaper reporters. It so happened that we had two 'characters' at the fishing (now sadly passed on to their last anchor-ages) who dearly loved to pull the legs of innocent tourists with tall tales, all in harmless fun. On these two worthies the reporters descended, all agog for 'copy'. 'As fishermen, what are your opinions of all this?', they asked.

That was enough, off they went in full blast. Wearing suitably solemn expressions, they explained to the reporters how much it was affecting them. 'We fishermen believe that when we die, our souls are transferred to seals'. 'Wow', said the reporters, 'what a story!', and forthwith in the papers came the earth-shaking announcement – 'Seahouses men believe they turn into seals when they die!'. We had a good laugh over this, so obviously a leg-pull.

There was a sequel a year or two later. Somebody, having visited the area, wrote something like this. 'When I arrived at Seahouses I found a busy fishing village with a fleet of modern boats, but was astonished to learn that the fishermen believed that, when they died, their souls were transmuted into seals'. From a pub joke, it had escalated into the realms of authenticity – because it had been down in black and white!.

Elsewhere it was said that Seahouses was a small port where some salmon fishing is done and a bit long-lining, provided they can get their wives to bait them for them. This at the time when we had our full fleet and lines had never been baited for over 30 years!.

'Ghost ship sails again!', I read. 'Seahouses fishermen afraid to put out in case they meet it as it carries on its ghostly way from island to island'. 'Giant seas scoop ship from the sea bottom where she has lain for 40 years!' Worthy of Edgar Allan Poe!

What with souls being transmuted into seals and then tales of ghost ships, people must think, 'they are a right funny lot, those Seahouses fishermen!'.

So lets tell you what I know about the so-called 'ghost ship'. The story relates to the great storm of January 1953, but it begins in 1916. The ship was the 3-master topsail schooner, the 'Spica', from Riga, Latvia. She was 300 tons and painted white. I remember seeing her from our harbour pier, ashore on the Wamses, two of the outer Farne Islands, in 1916, when I would be about five. She was laden with pit props and got among the maze of rocks in the dark, striking the North Wamses. It was fairly sheltered and she was then fast among broken rocks so she was unloaded of her cargo which was towed ashore by local cobles. They also removed most of the spars, sails and other salvable materials. As the hull lightened up, she moved farther up and south, finally coming to rest on a level spur of the South Wamses. It must have been a very high tide for her to get there, but there she was, bows and stern broken off, her sides fell out and the decks collapsed into the interior until she was nearly flat. Most of her length remained, the decks just like as if she were afloat. She lay like that for 40 years, and because her final resting place was even more sheltered, so she lay, undisturbed. In the nesting season, gulls nested in the shelter of the hatches.

Then came the great storm of January 1953, when parts of the east coast of England, and parts of Holland were flooded, causing many casualties. There was a huge tidal surge and winds of hurricane force. The combined height of the tide and the large seas were enough to shift her poor rotting carcase off the rock. Bits were were washed up on the islands and the mainland.

The story that she had been abandoned by her crew, sailing the North Sea for years, is incredible. The North Sea isn't that big. It is busy with cargo ships and fishing vessels, let alone how could it carry on thus through Hitler's war – and be within sight of Seahouses fishermen! I've heard of anglers' tales..........

There have been many wrecks in the area. The first I saw as a small child was that of the 'Lovespring', a 3-masted barque, wrecked at Annstead Rocks, just down the coast. But talking of distortions, I must write something about the Grace Darling story.

7.   GRACE DARLING.

Now Grace's youngest brother was George Darling. He was a ship's carpenter to trade, his early sea-going career being in the small sailing ships that carried on the coastal trade. He returned to fishing in later years, and as a young man, my grandfather, Richard Allen, was a crewman on George Darling's boat.

My great-grandfather was born in 1833, five years before the event. He died in 1921, when I was nine. So I had a personal connection through both. The story has been told to me many times. Many accounts of it have been written, many not accurate, the most authentic being written by Grace's elder sister, Thomasina, with the help of a professional writer. Emphasis was made in some of the writings of jealousy towards the Darlings by the local people, who were accused of belittling the whole affair. We read accounts

A 1930s view. The freighter is German, 'Hanna Holken', a regular visitor for barrels of salt herring.

produced when most of the people involved were still alive which were unable to fix the location of the 'Fern Islands', as they were then marked on the charts. We read also of Grace's father, William Darling's supposed cowardice in wanting to hold back. These make one despair!.

The account I refer to placed the 'Fern Islands' off St.Abbs Head, 30 miles north of their true position. Contemporary artists, working from hearsay mostly, produced some dramatic representations of the rescue. They were invariably in swirling heaps of salt water and in an area where Grace and her father never were, and could not have been. The accounts may be examined in Bamburgh Museum. Some have suggested that Grace went herself. There are drawings of her in an ordinary rowing boat, herself at the oars. The real boat was a coble, the same as used for fishing, and it may be seen in the museum. The Victorians were romantics, and in an era when young ladies were supposed to swoon at the slightest disturbance, and not to do things like Grace's effort, it seized the public imagination. All the ingredients were there for sensation – a lonely lighthouse on jagged island rocks, elderly parents, beautiful young maiden, fearful storm, raging seas, shipwreck, and pitiful survivors clinging to wave-washed rocks with the wreck looming over their head.

No wonder they seized on it with great avidity as it was better than all the stage plays they had seen.

The ship, the 'Forfarshire', had struck about or just after the height of the tide and she was lying at an angle to the rock in a shallow gulley with her bows pointing roughly east by north. Before she broke in two, some nine persons had succeeded in launching one of the small boats which were carried on each side aft. As the bulk of the ship formed a temporary breakwater, they were able to launch it successfully and scramble aboard. Before they could beach her on the rocks she was swept clear and rushed through the channel, the narrow Piper Gut, and so won clear into the lee of the complex of islands thereabout. In the dark they could not risk a landing and it was impossible to reach the lighthouse as all the intervening reefs were underwater. The sea was breaking heavily, so they had to run south before the wind, being picked up by a coaster miles to the south next morning. Had there been an ebb tide surging north through the Gut at the time of the launch, the boat would have been lost, but the latter part of the flood running south actually helped them. This event has often been ignored in the later drama when daylight appeared. Had more people gone to the ship's bows instead of remaining in the after saloon, more would have been saved.

As it was she parted just abaft of the paddle wheels, the after portion with its complement of people being swept into the deep water of the Piper Gut and sunk. The tide ebbed and the handful of crew and passengers scrambled, or were lowered, on to the rock from the now almost dry bows. They found a bit of shelter under the lee of a rock face, huddled together, and awaited the coming day. On the lighthouse, under half a mile seaward, the wreck had been observed early on, and as dawn strengthened, figures were seen moving about. The wind was easing, the tide getting well down, and William was assessing the chances of a rescue. He had a very limited choice of help, either his elderly wife, or a delicate young daughter, who even then had in her body the seeds of her early death, tuberculosis.

The small boat on which the success of the venture depended was moored afloat, not hauled up as some suggest, in a gully called 'Sunderland Hole'. That was fortunate, as had she been at the boat landing at the north of the lighthouse, she would have been hauled up and unable to be launched through lack of water and exposure to the elements.   The tale that the three Darlings launched the boat over the rocks is pure fiction. It is at least 100 yards from the boat landing to Sunderland Hole – the only logical launching site – over rough rocks which would have damaged the boat severely, apart from the fact that they hadn't the strength to do so. We have the supposed altercation between William and his wife and also for her scolding Grace for taking her father to his likely death. Ah, the pathos of it!. Mrs.Darling would more likely tell Grace to keep warm and dry!.

Sunderland Hole, being well down Crawford's Gut, was close to the nearest of the chain of island reefs running west to the Big Harcar where the wreck was lying. The only open water was about 100 yards across. At low water the shoal ground west of the lighthouse rock itself would be absorbing the broken seas. Crawford's Gut was therefore navigable. The reefs were well exposed, the tide ebbing, so away they went, Grace on the starboard oar, and William sitting on the seat forward of her on the port oar. This was to let Grace have the easier job, as William had to keep the boat's head from slewing with the wind. Getting across under the lee of the 'Bluecaps', they were immediately into sheltered water. They proceeded the rest of the way, keeping a safe distance, to the Little Harcars and so to the Big Harcars, all joined together at low water. Under the main height of the Big Harcars is a cleft in the cliff, as if made specially for a boat landing. Straight rock side and deep below, it makes an ideal landing place, especially with the wind on the other side of the island. William went on to the rock and would have taken a rope, made fast to the boat, with him. We don't know if he went inland to assist the survivors. If he did, he would have made the rope fast, with Grace remaining in the boat to stop it chafing against the rock with the rise and fall of the sea.

Taking the strongest of the sailors to assist, the women were got aboard the coble and they set off back to the lighthouse. A few were left behind as the boat was unable to hold them all at once. Grace had done all that was required of her, the sailors helping her father to row the boat. The transfer, via Sunderland Hole again, was successfully accomplished, William and a sailor setting back for

70

the rest of the survivors. This trip was also done without incident. By then the tide was on the flow but the wind had moderated with a consequent fall in the breaking seas.

While all this was taking place, keen eyes, four miles away on the mainland, had seen the ship's foremast which was still standing. With the tide making and the wind and the sea moderating, some hardy souls from the fishing community of Seahouses set out in a coble to see if they could help. As at the launch of the quarter boat, the significance of this escaped the historians. Some accounts say the lifeboat could not be launched; some say it was launched, which is indeed peculiar, as there was no lifeboat at Seahouses until nearly 20 years later!. The names of the coble's crew are known and at least one of Grace's brothers was amongst them. On reaching the Harcars they landed and brought off the body of an old Minister of the Gospel, and the bodies of the two bairns, taking them to the lighthouse. All had died from exposure. As the wind freshened again, they decided to wait it out. They had to remain storm bound for a few days until boats could get off to the sea again.

After the survivors had returned to the mainland and a short time elapsed, the story broke – Grace was the nation's toast! 'The Heroine of the North', and so forth, was the lighthouse keeper's daughter. Songs were composed and people went 'Grace Darling daft!'.

The outcome of all this unwarranted publicity was to cause the Darlings acute embarrassment. They were not used to this sort of adulation. William, himself, said he could never figure out what all the fuss was about. To the Darlings and to the local people it was nothing out of the ordinary. Wrecks and rescues were a feature of the coast every winter. Many heroic deeds were performed and went unremarked and unrecorded. When a reporter quizzed local people and did not get the reaction he was seeking, he wrote that the locals were jealous of the Darlings, which was not true.

William Darling said later that of all the pictures he saw of the rescue only one remotely resembled the real thing. I read some time ago a suggestion that Grace deliberately exaggerated her ailment because she wanted to avoid any more fuss, and in the process, hastened her own demise. This was a most unfair slur on her. It was all very analytical and auto–suggestive, making much of Grace's cough. The girl was in an advanced state of tuberculosis, and well into a terminal decline, the doctors of the day not having the knowledge to deal with it. To those theorists I say, 'leave the poor lassie to rest in peace.'

I have given the true account; the bare facts as handed down from one generation to another. As Northumbrians we are justly proud of Grace – and her family – but deplore what has been wrongly applied to all who took part in the rescue.

One further word. There was usually a gale from a northerly direction about the end of August or into September every year. They were not the tremendous gales as attributed to the story. There would be a sharp, severe, blow, lasting overnight and into the next morning, enough to raise a nasty sea but not enormous breakers. I have seen many such in my lifetime. Just after the last war two boats were herring fishing out the 'North Side' and were caught out in the same sort of blow. One was local, one from the Firth. The local boat told the other to follow closely as it was a flood tide running through the Piper Gut into shallow water, with the breaking sea a few yards on either side. The situation was much the same as the 'Forfarshire'. Not a howling hurricane but enough to wreck the ship because she stranded.

8.   IN LIGHTER VEIN.

In describing life in the village years ago, if I have given the impression that there was little laughter, or more kicks than ha'pence, then I apologise. Over the years we appreciated a good joke. They are remembered and can still be laughed at.

Like all villages then, we had our local characters. There was always someone who stood out from the crowd by means of wit or the ability to find an occasion to create a laughable situation. One such I remember was a natural. During the first war, when rationing was a new experience, he said to his wife one day when he was getting his dinner, 'hand me ma glasses, lass'.

'Wat ye want yer glasses for?, she asked, 'its time ye were gan back tae work, no read the paper'.

'Ah want me glasses so these dam' rations'll look a bit bigger!'.

In one of the houses near to the Bamburgh Castle Inn was a free surgery every Friday run by a charity for the poor. I recall going several times and seeing square glass medicine bottles stuck on pegs, at a 45 degree angle, to dry. Somehow the medicine was always

My Uncle, John Allen, taken in early 1960s, then aged 75. I started as a fisherman with him.

the same colour and smell and tasted like peppermint. One of the local bairns used to take her Granny's medicine over to Beadnell, two miles away, every Saturday, picking up the empty on return. This day she was playing with the bottle when she tripped. The bottle fell out of her hands on to the grass at the roadside, the cork came out, and half the contents were lost. Being a resourceful bairn she topped it up at the burn which flowed down to the sea a short distance away. Now the water was brackish, half salt, a pale colour like weak tea and flavoured with decomposing seaweed. She duly delivered it, got the empty and returned home. Next Saturday when she went, Granny said, 'tell the doctor ah want the medicine like last weeks, its the best ah've ivver had, ahm like a new wummin!' Such is the power of faith!.

The latrines for the harbour were primitive affairs, a concrete structure built out over the sea wall opposite the present lifeboat house. They consisted of two long passages, the outer open to the sky, the other, containing half a dozen cubicles, had a roof. To perform a major biological function (hows that for a mouthful), it was needful to stick ones stern over the open hole in the cubicle. Medieval castles had much the same idea! It was also rather gloomy inside. Well, this day a couple of men from an Eyemouth boat were doing the necessary when into the exterior passage came a summer visitor for a pee. In warm weather it could pong a bit, so he said aloud, thinking he was alone, 'What a hell of a smell!', whereupon a disembodied voice from the other side piped up, 'Whit dae ye think we s##t, mate, scented soap?.' A bit basic but funny for all that!

Another time I was sitting with my pal alongside some of the older generation one late afternoon in summer. The old 'uns were smoking their pipes and yarning quietly when across came a couple of young 'townies'. They were trying to boost a newspaper by going about canvassing and were real eager-beavers, full to the hatches with sales patter. They fixed their attention on one of the old 'uns who was puffing away at his old clay cutty and asked, 'do you take a daily paper?'.

'Aye', says he. 'Oh', said the young un, 'you should try ours', the paper that, according to the patter, was the most read, respected, etc. 'Oh, aye', said the old 'un, what paper wid that be, now?'. The 'Daily Mail', came the answer. 'What paper do you take?', 'The Daily Mail', said the old 'un. The lad was a bit nonplussed after all his wasted patter, and said, 'how long have you taken it?'. When the old timer said, 'since the Boer War', the lad, weeping hysterically, was led away by his mate!.

My grandfather in his latter days lived with my aunt and uncle. One evening when she and her husband were going out for an hour or two, said to him, 'we'll be oot for a bit, but we'll be back aboot 9 so git yer own supper'. 'Righto', he said, 'aa kin fend for mesel a' right'. When she returned she said to the old man, 'what did ye hev for yer supper?'. 'Some cheese an' n'onion'. She thought, 'that's funny, there's nae onions in the hoose', and asked, 'where did ye git them fra?'. 'Offen the shelf in the back kitchen'. She looked at the shelf and two of her hyacinth bulbs had gone!. He managed to live to 85.

At a hotel overlooking the harbour, a new cocktail bar had been installed, to be opened in a glare of publicity. A visiting gaggle of priests and a Bishop were having a conference in the village at the time. They all came trooping down the bank to the harbour where a dozen or so of the local worthies were sitting. The Bishop paused in front of them and said, 'I suppose you'll all be waiting for the big event, the opening of the new bar?'. An old worthy got stiffly to his feet, 'now look here, me man', he said, 'd'ye see 'aa these men here?'. 'If ye cud find two that drinks, ye'll be lucky!'. Collapse of Bishop!.

I have often read how Americans poke fun at we British for having only a small island as our homeland – and how the 'whistle stop' Americans belt around at full throttle. One day I was on the jetty at the Inner Farne Island when a boat discharged her lot of tourists. A couple approached me and in unmistakeable American accents asked if I were a local. On replying, yes, the man said, 'could you come around with us and point out anything of interest that we might otherwise miss?. So, off we went, me explaining that it was the island where St.Cuthbert had lived his last days and died. He was busy writing all this down in longhand, so when I stopped to let him catch up, his wife told me they had been in England – in London for three years, as he was a 'perfessor' at some University. I didn't get to learn what he 'perfessed'. Half way round she suddenly grabbed his arm and said, 'hurry up, Elmer, we've only another twenty minutes'. She turned to me and said, ' we're going to Edinburgh tomorrow, and doing Scatland the next day!'. Whether she thought that 'Scatland' was a little patch of ground outside of Edinburgh I never got to know!.

9.   THE NORTHUMBRIAN COBLE.

Numerous writers have pondered, speculated and agonised over the origins, peculiarities and description of this unique boat. Artists have tried to depict them, but few have really succeeded in capturing their elusive lines. In fact, the only straight lines they possess are the 'thofts', the 'thwarts' or seats, the name coming from athwart ships, i.e. across the breadth or beam.

No two have ever been built exactly alike, they are strictly one–off jobs. So, where did they originate, who invented them and why were they built in that remarkable fashion?.

My first introduction to the sea was in a pulling and sailing coble as a very small boy. I started life as a fisherman in one, although by

*A '3 planked' sailing coble, the 'Emperor', in 1905.
Seated is my Great Uncle, Bob Rutter.
Standing is my Grandfather, Richard Allen, Senr.*

that time they had small engines but were still rigged for sail.

Lets start at the very beginning with the name 'Coble'. I am not going to argue about the origin of the word as in my mind it is irrelevant to the description. Various theories have been propounded, but they agree loosely that it means 'boat'. The Celtic orientated theorists contend that the shape was derived, and I quote, 'probably from coracles', without there being any evidence to that effect. How the Bronze and Iron Age lads got about in this district I will not venture to say. Was it skin-covered baskets or dug-outs like the one found at Barton-on-Humber?.

It has also been said that the coble is a planked version of the Irish curragh. Now, bonny lads, which one?. Because there are two. The only representation of one is from a gold model made centuries ago, shaped like a bath with rounded ends, and made from wickerwork covered in hides. Similar ones, but canvas covered, were used on the west coast of Ireland at least before the last war. They were paddled by a peculiar spade-shaped paddle. The other one, the Galway Bay curragh of lath and canvas, was shaped like half an empty mussel shell, round bottom, narrow beam, cocked up bow, and so unstable that each rower had to use two oars to act as 'outriggers' to stop it capsizing. The fact that it was used in poor sea conditions gave rise to the idea that they were remarkable sea boats. The plain fact is that it was only due to the skill of the men who handled them that they managed at all. They were and are a very primitive form of boat, but, because they are light, they are able to be beached and lifted clear of the water easily. Celtic theorists maintain that this was the inspiration for the first cobles and contend that they were brought to our coast by Irish missionaries. This latter point and the fact the the outline of the Galway curragh with its 'cocky up bow' is evidence in their minds, then let me dissect that conclusion.

1. I cannot find a shred of evidence, in writing or illustration, to the missionary theory. In any case they came to a land peopled with skilled builders of wooden boats who would scorn the idea of copying a skin−covered basket.
2. There is no evidence that the Galway model even existed then.
3. The trap of falling into the 'comparative outline' theory for this is exceedingly thin ice indeed. The Galway curraghs' bow was not immersed in the water, it was a high bow.
4. The coble, which has the appearance of a high bow when grounded, has actually a deep bow; the bow and stern roughly the same height when the boat is afloat.

If we are to accept the comparative outline theory, then the Polynesian 'Proas', the Red Indian canoes, the Venetian gondolas and the Norse longships must have all originated from the same source, as all had upflung stems and sterns. Let us examine the method of coble construction i.e. plank over plank, the clench, or clinker or lap−strake method. This was the way the people of the north built their boats from the very early days, probably starting with a dug−out, like the Barton on Humber boat, but with added planks per side to heighten the hull − as simple as that!.

The Celts, talented people though they were, never got even to that primitive stage nor were they much to the fore in practical inventions. Their talents were more to be found in song and stories of bygone heroes, giants, fairies, etc. Their skin−covered baskets were their sole contribution to the maritime world. They have lasted through the centuries because they were incapable of improvement. When, finally, they got around to constructing 'proper' vessels, they were invariably copies of those produced by other more advanced maritime builders. The theorists of the Celtic related argument may well recoil at this challenge to their findings – 'the man isn't even a scholar!'. I rest my case!

The oldest and best example of an Anglo-Saxon built vessel was that found at Nydam, in north Germany and whose description is well recorded. She exhibits no example of outstanding importance, but is a simple design of broad planks, lapped and clenched. She has a long, narrow hull, is very sharp in the floors, low in the midships, and rising gradually to the pointed bow and stern. She was for rowing only, being too 'tender' to sail. The remains of the Sutton Hoo ship were only the imprints of the planks and the rusted marks where iron nails were used in the plank fastenings. The outline was so well excavated that it was possible to see that the uprise of the planking was very similar to the Nydam ship, albeit larger. They were two examples of the early Anglo-Saxon model but they laid the foundations for the method of building. As they gained more experience so vessels improved, particularly those subject to critical assessment through daily use on the open sea.

Take a long, thin, straight softwood plank, clamp it with one end horizontal to the ground, and twist the other into a vertical position and you've made the first step in building a boat. A plank twisted in such a manner will curve and come up at the vertical end, so the embryo sheer was in being. To get the subsequent planking to conform to shape, it had to be curved along its length, and the ends – if it ran full length – had to be narrower than the centre width. It was found that a boat was safer when driven into the sea were it higher at each end. Further, the sheer added lateral strength to the fabric. The keel, the backbone of the vessel, was given a curve because a long keel in a straight section of a longish boat tended to develop an upward curve in the centre thus transmitting the fault even to the upper topsides. This was known as 'hogging'. Early Nordic builders discovered this at a very early stage in their boat building.

It was the men who sailed them who were responsible for new ideas, explaining to the builders what they wanted. Progress was by trial and error. Until fairly modern times, a fisherman would tell the builder of his new boat that he would like to have this or that alteration which he considered an advance on the current model.

The clench build was light and strong but as size increased the

A '4 planked coble, the 'Boy's Pride', owner H.Rutter, taken in the 1920s, after conversion from sail to motor.

problems also increased. In a seaway they did not remain rigid, but 'worked', twisting and moving to the pressure of lift and drop of the seas. If too rigid they would split, so a method was evolved in that they were allowed a fraction of movement of the timber, allowing it to spring and bend. Instead of nailing the planks – the skin of the ship – to the ribs, they lashed them with lashings across the ribs to eyes formed inside the plank when it was made.

To make a plank they split the tree trunk all along its length in the centre, using iron wedges. The resultant flat edges were adzed level. The plank was laid face down and the curved side divided into lengths by marks on the wood. Where each timber was to lie they cut a piece out, leaving a semi–circular piece beside the next timber slot. They eventually got a plank flat with half round pieces at each timber, through which half circle holes were bored.

Now in a clench built boat the skin of the boat is first built up with the planks all 'sewn' along their edges with the clench nails, the timbers then shaped to fit on the planks on the inside of the hull. The Norse method was to pass lashings over and over the timber and through the holes in the side pieces as described. Although it served its purpose it was not a good method at bottom for the lashings were subject to the vagaries of the weather and must have been constantly in need of attention. The Norsemen had two classes of ships, one, the ocean going cargo carrier, beamy, big, and strong, were called 'Knorir'. The more familiar long, or dragon, ship, the warship, was leaner for easy rowing and under sail.

The popular conception of a huge fearsome dragon's head rising high on a slender stem piece must be taken with a grain of salt. Made of wood, and subject to the weight thereof, they would have to conform to a certain size, so that no undue strain was placed on the stem piece. The only example to survive was like a leopard's head without ears and of a reasonable size. The figureheads as depicted in most of the films were enormous, but, being made of plastic, did not strain the stem. The Nordics hadn't plastic, they just had to make do with wood!.

While thinking about films, when I see a costume film of olden times and the actors are earning their keep, it always amazes me to see they appear to be wearing clothes straight from the tailors. Was not the real thing that people were were dressed in work−worn, dirty, often filthy, clothes. They were rarely washed, were flea bitten, and unkempt with even the gentry not being overly hygienic and smelling to high heaven!.

When the Angles crossed the North Sea they took the shortest route, down the Dutch coast and across where it was fairly narrow, as their boats were more for rowing than sailing. The primitive square sail was universal in the northern hemisphere. Sails did not advance in design as did the ships, fair wind, up sail, adverse wind, out oars. It was many years before the art of sailing was practised but, gradually, a concept of using that square of cloth or leather to the best advantage came into being.

When the wind, instead of being directly astern, hauled more to her side, someone took the weather tack forward, bowsing it down tight, the lee tack eased off a trifle and taken a bit more aft, and lo, there she was, moving through the sea as well as if the wind had changed. From this evolved the familiar lug sail, the simple, loose−footed, efficient motive power machine to drive a boat, using wind power, and able to do so from almost all angles except dead ahead. Such a sail was that of the Coble.

Suppose we are a newly arrived clan of immigrants from Saxony or south Denmark. Our landing place is between Tweed and Tyne. It is a coast of sandy beaches and rocky headlands, lacking natural harbours except maybe Holy Island. The water is shallow and thus subject to much wave activity. The boats used for the crossing had to be big enough to carry the people, their household goods, tools, livestock and so on to start a new life. Undoubtedly they would be at least 50 feet long and double-ended. Likely too, they would tow a small rowing skiff. Their ship is grounded in shelter in a cove. They start to unload provided no problem comes from the local Britons. The embryo settlement is begun and well under way when the weather worsens. The big boat is in danger so they set to with man and animal power to haul her up clear of the high water mark where she lies.

Later, and after the village has been established, somebody fancies a codling for their supper and, finding the skiff too small, casts a calculating look at the big boat. 'She's too heavy to get up and launch each trip, so why not half her?', they think. By adding a transom to each of the severed ends, they could have two handy boats of 25 feet, useful for fishing and only half as heavy.

Knowing what makes the Nordic mind tick, I would not be surprised if this did not happen!.

A boat should always be beached head to the sea unless she is double-ended. So there we have the beginning, sharp bow to the sea, flat transom to beach. Follow my reasoning?. It is found that the flat stern actually prevents an easy beaching as it pushes a ridge of water before it when the boat is brought end on, clear of the breaking seas. It also digs into the land when actually touching. The remedy? Give the stern a slope of 45º!. Instant success!. All the men within a reasonable distance hear about it and come and have a look. So all new boats are built thus.

This was not done overnight. Many moons and years had to pass while they made do. One day somebody beaching his boat had her knocked broadside on to the beach, capsized, and badly damaged. The cause was simple. She drew the same amount of water all along her length, so when the stern was aground, the bow was still afloat on the sloping sand. The remedy here was that the bow was made deeper, so that, when she grounded, it was all along her bottom, holding her firm. Brilliant!. More examination of the new model, maybe at first with a false forefoot nailed on to increase the grip, the ever resourceful boat builder considered how to make the forefoot as he constructed a new hull.

It was a logical progression by trial and error and an awareness of how to get on. There was a parallel a few years ago. Introduction

A '5 planked' motor coble, the 'Clan Gillean', after she was sold to a Craster fisherman.

of the motor into the cobles in the 1920s presented the problem of how to get a shaft and propellor from the engine to under the after part of the flat after-hull. The solution?. A clog of wood on the inside of the ram plank, i.e. the middle bottom plank between the twin keels, with another clog on the outside. A stern tube hole then bored at an angle from the engine to the propellor through the clogs, a universal joint on the shaft just aft of the under clog packing gland on the stern tube. This shaft to go aft below to a bearing supported by a vertical shaft which could be pulled up. This brought the two-bladed propeller to rest tight up between the two parallel keels, the 'droughts' (drowts) to be out of the way when the coble grounded. The engine had to be stopped or out of gear to do this. The most recent development not many years ago, was in order to do away with the chore of pulling up the propeller every time. It was fixed to a shorter shaft, a cavity being formed under the bottom for the prop. to run in. The two-bladed prop was replaced by a three bladed, and the droughts deepened a bit to give a higher rise to the coble's bottom, when grounded, to protect the now-fixed propellor.

So we have a boat with the underwater body conforming to the slope of the landing beach. Protection for the vulnerable bottom planks was achieved by adding hardwood runners with iron plates to stop wear. The forefoot keel, which came from the bows to half way aft on to the ram centre plank, was also shod. The early broad planked boats lent themselves to a particularly pleasing contour. From the outside bottom plank edge, the first plank to come up to form the sides was known as the 'first riser'. It came up at a shallow angle, but the next riser was vertical. The upper plank was turned inboard sharply to give an angled half-round side, like the letter 'C'. This form of side served two important purposes. It kept the boat drier when lying over to sail pressure and much increased the lateral strength of the lightly-built hull. Looking from above, the shape was, by then, long since departed from the original crude half boat!. The stern was much narrower, the sides from bow to stern flowing in a sweet curve, in fact the final shape was in the lines of this boat.

The inventive brains were hard at work, the product of centuries of boat building know-how. The old methods were still used, the timbers curved and rebated to fit. The inside plank edges are now nailed. Around the outside of the top plank is a strong piece of hard -wood i.e, the gunwhale, or gunnel. Thwarts (thofts) to set and row on also keep the boat rigid across her beam. Sophistication was creeping in!.

The art of beaching a coble stern first was to turn the boat head to sea outside the breakers, an oar out on each side. Shades of the Old Norse steering oar on the starboard 'steer-board' quarter. There was a thole pin on the coble's quarter, but on the port side. An oar was put on it, the long rudder taken off and shipped aboard. In she went, assisted by the run of the sea, kept moving by the midship oars, and steered by the quarter oar. There was another use for this oar and thole pin which is explained further on. As we are on the subject of oars, I must explain that there was a difference between the Yorkshire oars and those used by we Northumbrians. We had for the main rowing oars, depending on the size of the coble, averaging about 16 feet long, all one piece of spruce. When they were outboard in the rowing position so much oar projected into the boat that the rower had to sit on the far side of the 'thoft'. This was a balance of forces, the long 'loom' of the oar from the thole pin to the rower compensating for the remaining 10 feet of oar on the outside, 5 feet of which was the long narrow blade. One man could not row two of these oars at once, the looms resembling a St.Andrews cross in the centre of the boat. Oh, it could be done after a fashion, but what an awkward performance rowing with your arms crossed!. In summer it was sometimes necessary, when all the lads were at the herring, and the old men and boys in the cobles were a bit short of manpower. Then, they used a pair of oars designed to be used by one man. It was all done cleverly. The 'hands' of the oar just cleared on meeting in the boat's centre, the balance being kept by making the oar in two sections. The inboard piece was of softwood, spruce, larch or pine; the blade of the outboard section usually of ash, and with a very thin cross-section. This inboard end was broad and thick with a 'hand', like a horn, at the end to get your fingers around. The ash blade was screwed and lashed up the foreside of the softwood piece and there it was, a combination of counter balances to make the tiring operation of rowing as easy as possible. Lifeboat oars had lead plugs inserted in the inboard sections for counterbalance.

I have not had much contact with the Yorkshire layout. It was different from ours although the boats were basically the same. In my view there were major and minor points to show that our set up was more efficient. My object is to describe the boats I was born amongst and just generalise about the Yorkshire ones. I do not know if the Yorkies used the long sweeps. All the oars I ever saw in their boats were the double-wooded ones — we called them 'paddles'. If you have managed to follow me so far, I hope you have, then we have progressed another step towards the realisation of why and how the cobles were invented, one of the methods of their propulsion, and how they achieved the objective of what they were designed for, namely, safe beaching on shallow coasts.

The early days of the 19C were a very ticklish time for the coastal fishermen. They had been engaged in illegal enterprises for a very long time. At the same time they were at the mercy of the Naval Press Gangs who would grab all and sundry of the coastal young men to fill their warships. There, life for the unfortunate lower deck rating was hell on earth, so they fought back the only way they could against authority — by smuggling contraband. The coble was an ideal boat for this. At that time the small cobles had no outer stem piece, the planks coming to a sharp edge over the inner 'deadwood' to which they were nailed. The easily damaged planking was protected by a sheet of copper, beaten around the stem, as with Grace Darling's little coble in Bamburgh Museum. I have not seen any paintings or models prior to the late 1700s. Since most small boats had conventional outer stem pieces, it is not beyond the bounds of possibility that some larger cobles would be constructed thus. The nearest I can find is a pencil or ink drawing by the Tyneside artist Charles Henry Napier, 1841–1917, of French antecedents who painted spirited pictures of fishermen and boats in Cornwall and Devon. The drawing I refer to was entitled 'Salmon boats' and would be done when in his late teens. It is very well detailed, a three–quarter view from aft, but exhibiting several peculiarities. The other boat in the picture is like an ordinary square–sterned, or wine glass stern, that is common everywhere. The coble is a four planker four up from the last flat one. She has a short deck stretching from the fore thoft to the stem, and some indeterminate spars laid fore and aft, which could be oars and mast. She appears to have been roughly repaired on both sides by the addition of planks nailed to the existing ones. She also displays an addition to her normal transom, which could be described as an oval with a flattened top and bottom.

This addition suggests to me that she has been sold 'foreign', further down the coast because I have never come across the like of it in 'coble country'. It resembles a, say two inch thick, piece of wood, from the bottom of the transom to the top, the bottom broad, but tapering to very thin at the top, so that the sharp rake of the transom is neutralised. It appears to have gudgeons for rudder pintles on it, so that a rudder would hang almost vertical instead of conforming to the usual 45° slope. Nevertheless it is undoubtedly a proper coble. Thus, by c.1858, we had four planked cobles, and a proper stern!.

We come to the latter part of the 19C when cobles had reached the peak of their being. Sail was on the way out for ocean–going ships, but still king in most fishing fleets. Steam was attracting a lot of interest. Internal combustion was yet in its most primitive form and it would be another two decades before they were installed in some of the larger keelboats and Zulus, indeed not until the 20s in Seahouses boats.

The coble under sail was a lively, fast, and weatherly boat. By the long, easy lines it took little to force her through the water. In the hands of men who had sailed them all their lives, they came through

The Northumbrian Sailing Coble No. 1.

INTERIOR PLAN LAYOUT.

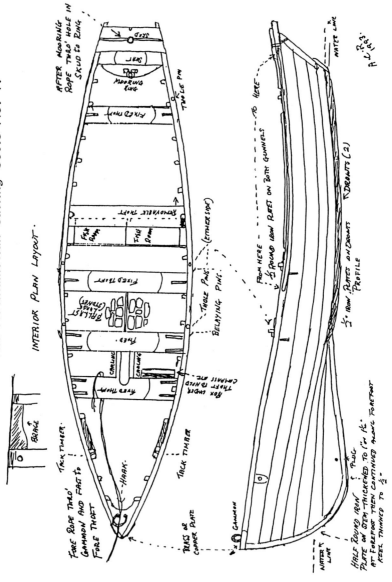

BRACE

THICK TIMBER

FORE ROPE THRO' GAMMON AND FAST TO FORE THOFT

AFTER MOORING ROPE THRO' HOLE IN SKUD TO RING

SKED

SEAT

MOORING RING

FIXED THOFT

THOLE PIN

REMOVABLE THOFT

FISH POUND

FISH ROOM

THOLE PINS (EITHER SIDE)

BELAYING PINS

FIXED THOFT

BALLAST LONG STONES

FIXED

CEILING

CEILING

BOX UNDER THOFT TO HOLD CEMENT ETC.

FIXED THOFT

HOOK

TACK TIMBER

BRASS OR COPPER PLATE

GAMMON

WATER LINE

FROM HERE

TO HERE

⅝ ROUND IRON PLATES ON BOTH GUNNELS

½" IRON PLATES ON DRAUGHT PROFILE

DRAUGHTS (2)

WATER LINE

A.L.R.G.3.

WATER LINE

HALF ROUND IRON ⅝ DIA. PLATE ON STEM THICKENED TO 1" ½. AT FOREFOOT THEN CONTINUED ALONG FOREFOOT KEEL THINNED TO ½"

86

The Northumbrian Sailing Coble No.2.

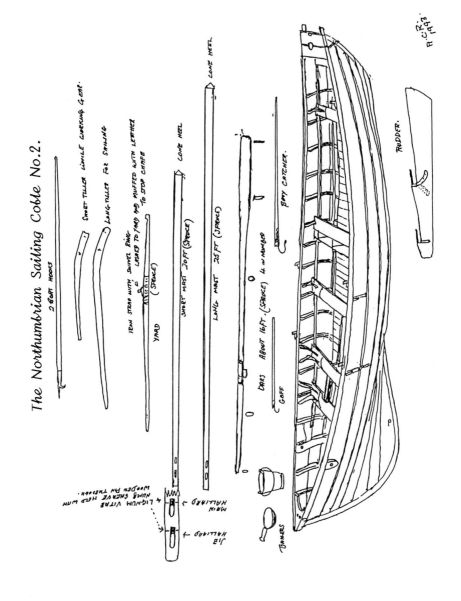

2 BOAT HOOKS

SHORT TILLER WHILE WORKING GEAR.

LONG TILLER FOR SAILING.

IRON STRAP WITH SWIVEL RING.
LASHED TO YARD AND MUFFLED WITH LEATHER
TO STOP CHAFE

YARD. (SPRUCE)

SHORT MAST 20FT (SPRUCE)

COME HEEL

LONG MAST 26 FT. (SPRUCE)

COME HEEL

BUOY CATCHER.

OARS ABOUT 16 FT. (SPRUCE) 4 IN NUMBER

GAFF

RUDDER.

JIB HALLIARD →

MAIN HALLIARD →

4 LIGNUM VITAE NUMB SHEAVE HELD WITH WOODEN PIN THROUGH.

BAILERS

R.C.R. 1943.

87

The Northumbrian Sailing Coble No.3.

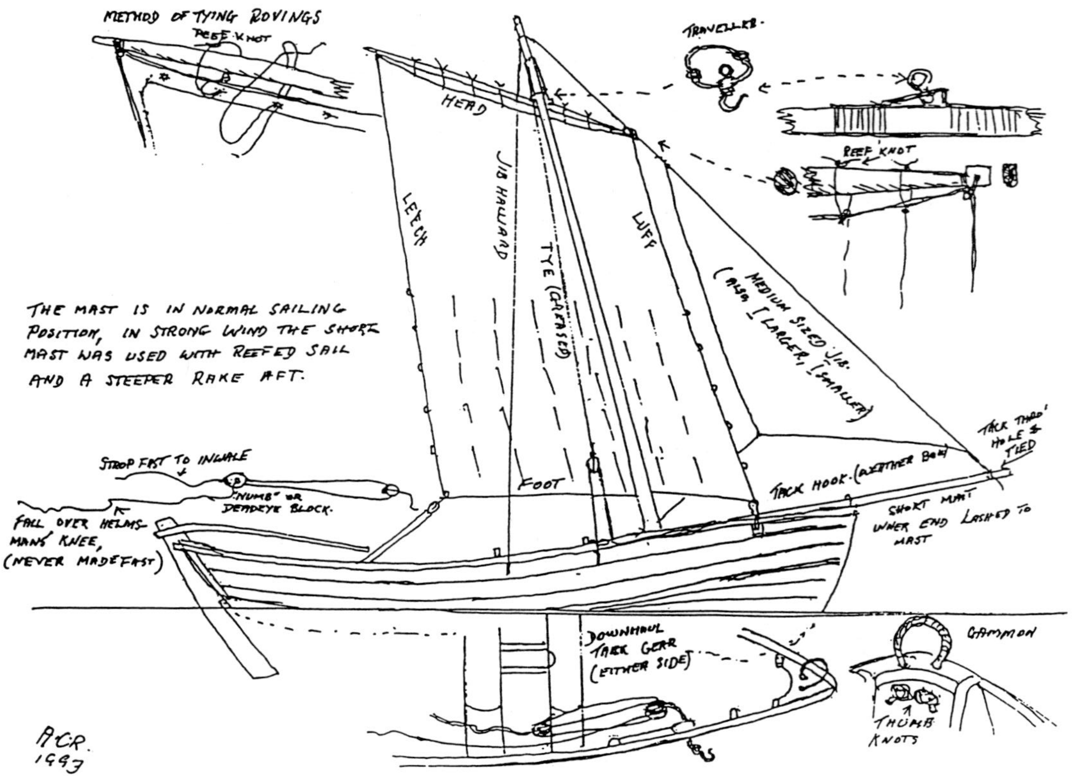

METHOD OF TYING ROVINGS
REEF KNOT

THE MAST IS IN NORMAL SAILING
POSITION, IN STRONG WIND THE SHORT
MAST WAS USED WITH REEFED SAIL
AND A STEEPER RAKE AFT.

STRAP FAST TO INHALE

"SWING" OR
DEADEYE BLOCK.

FALL OVER HELMS-
MANS KNEE,
(NEVER MADEFAST)

TRAVELLER

REEF KNOT

MEDIUM SIZED JIB
(ALSO 1 LARGER, 1 SMALLER)

LUFF

TYE (GREASED)

JIB HALLIARD

HEAD

LEECH

FOOT

TACK HOOK (EITHER BOW)

TACK TRAD.
7 HOLES
WHEN TIED

SHORT MAST
WHEN END LASHED TO
MAST

DOWNHAUL
TACK GEAR
(EITHER SIDE)

CHAMPION

A THUMB
KNOTS

ACR.
1993

some fearsome weather unscathed. Some, inevitably, were lost, but mostly when coming to land. At one time airtight wooden boxes were fitted in them so, if they filled, they would remain afloat. It was a sensible arrangement but took a lot of room. Only about 50% of the boats had them at the finish.

We come now to the last development of all, the sail. That piece of cloth which, in the layman's eye, is hung from a spar up the mast to belly with the wind and shove the boat along. Some may think that any bit of rag will do, not so. For centuries the universal sail was square, but it was discovered that cunning alterations to the cut and set made a tremendous difference to its efficiency. In short, technology was being applied to the sail as it had been to the hull. One thing complemented the other. The sails carried by our boats consisted of mainsail, or foresail, a small three-cornered jib, or a medium sized one, and in summer, a large one, reaching almost mast high. The mainsail, roughly rectangular and set longways up, was broader in the 'foot' than the 'head' which angled up from the edge or 'luff' of the sail to the 'lee' or 'leech', the trailing edge of the sail. The 'leech' was longer than the 'luff' and the top of the sail, the 'head', culminated at the corner where it met the 'leech' at the 'peak'. The edges of the sails were sewn to ropes to prevent them tearing across and down. On both 'luffs' and 'leeches' were iron thimbles called 'cringles' lashed on at spaced intervals, coinciding with the 'reef points'. These were short pieces of light cordage inserted at each panel sewing of the sail and hanging a foot or more on each side. They were to gather in the foot of the sail to reduce the area. In the average coble they had five or six rows from the bottom upwards.

The sails were of cotton, tanned in boiling 'cutch', a brown extract made from tree sap from the far east, 'Burmese cutch it was called. It was customary to soak the cotton in sea water before immersion in the cutch as this fastened in the dye. Tallow was also added to waterproof the cloth, making it also soft and supple. Both sails and herring nets were dipped to kill bacteria. The 'yard', the spar from which the sail hung, was tapered towards each extremity. The 'luff' end had a piece notched out about two inches from the end to hold the lashing which held the sail. The 'peak' end had just a hole through which to take the lashing. Along the 'head' of the sail, on the canvas where it was doubled into a broad hem, at each panel, was a small hole, finished with a sail-twine buttonhole stitch.

89

Through these small holes passed short pieces of small cord doubled, so they could be parted around the yard and tied, without binding the sail to the yard.

The sail hung four or five inches below the yard. About a third of the way from the 'luff' end was an iron strap about two and a half inches wide, beaten slightly concave on its lower surface. In its centre it contained a stout iron ring on which was formed an uprise. As the ring had to turn and swivel, it was bound to the yard by lashings of small cord, painted with preservative. To save the lashings from chafing through the mast, it had an old leather sea-boot leg laced over it, with the iron ring projecting clear. There were two masts, one the length of the boat, the other three quarters of the length of the long one. The short mast, which did duty as a bowsprit, was set only in very strong winds with a heavily reefed sail, when, of course, the long mast became the bowsprit!.

The 'heels', or bottoms, of both masts were cone-shaped to allow a mast to turn in its socket when the sail was shifted from one side to the other. The tops of the masts were flat and, starting 6/7 inches down from the top, a 1½ by 4 inch slot was bored, with another below. The masts, being of spruce or pine, were softwood, so the bases of the slots were protected by half-round sheaves of lignum vitae, a very hard wood. They did not rotate but were fixed in by a wooden peg driven through from one side of the masthead to the other. The masthead was usually white for 2-3 feet, the rest blue, while the yard was blue with white ends.

To hoist the sail, a well-greased rope ran over the lower sheave. The upper sheave was for the jib halliards. The greasy rope was called the 'tye', the sheave holes always fore and aft. The tye on the fore side of the mast came down to the 'traveller', an iron ring in two parts around the mast, the two parts joined on each side in rings rather like two pail handles joined at their rings. This was so the ring did not bind on the mast in setting or lowering as a rigid ring could do. At the centre of the diameter of the outer ring was formed a thick section with a swivelling ring and stout hook below. The tye was passed through the ring and a simple 'thumb' knot was used as a stopper to hold it. Chafing between the ring and tye was protected by a leather strip cut on one side into strips like a comb. When wrapped around the tye behind the knot these fringes splayed around the iron ring, very neat and tidy!. The downhaul end of the tye was bent on to a biggish single sheaved block, through which

90

passed the main halliards, one end culminating in an iron hook, the other whipped to stop it fraying.

That's the set up before we hoist the sail, and now we have the two lower corners of the sail to attend to. Four feet aft of the stem, on each 'shoulder' of the boat, is a very thick, broad timber. It is the strongest one of the lot, tapering as as it goes downwards. On the outside of the plank opposite to the timber head is a hardwood clog from the underside of the gunnel down, or nearly down, to the plank edge. Bored through from outside to in is a hole c.1½ inches in diameter through which goes a short greased tye – on both sides of the bows. On the outboard end of the tye is a large iron hook; on the inboard, a smallish double-sheaved block, the whole tye being only two feet or a little more in length. A single-sheaved block sits opposite the double-sheaved one, the downhaul halliard reeved through the two blocks, making a simple 'purchase'. On the single block a short strip of rope is tied to the 'inwale' or 'stringer' or 'inwaver', as we call it, just aft of the after fore thoft.

Righto! – remember all this, for now we are going to the other lower corner of the sail, the 'clew', to which is attached the sheet, the most important rope of the lot!. It is the one that controls the whole sail when on the move. A single sheave block is tied on the 'clew cringle', a pear-shaped numb or dead-eye block, i.e. one without a sheave, with a three foot tail strop around it. The sheet itself is spliced into the arc of the strop, the sheet to the clew block and through, thence back to the hole in the numb block and thence to the steersman. A stopper knot is in the loose end of the sheet in case it gets out of the block. The tail strop is made fast to the 'inwaver' on the lee side, well aft.

Now, me lads, we'll have her hoisted!.

The sail is flaked out on the lee side of the mast, the yard ring on to the traveller hook, and the luff cringle on to the downhaul hook on the weather shoulder. The hook on the main halliard is inserted into a cringle in a bight of rope on the inwale, aft of the mast position, and up she goes, hauling down on the single rope of the halliard. The sail is mastheaded, for the present the clew is left flapping. The halliard is passed under the prong of the belaying pin, which sits below the gunnel just in front of the fore thole pin. A loop in the halliard, or bight, is passed between the taut halliard and the outside gunnel. This is held by its own 'nip', a quick jerk will release it. Now the reason for the set up on the 'luff' cringle is

91

apparent, the short tye is at its most outboard extremity, the hook about a foot or more above the gunnel. So the tackle is hove short, the hook is hauled flush with the gunnel, thus tightening the luff rope(leading rope) of the sail as taut as possible. This increases the efficiency of the set of the sail.

To set the jib, the single halliard from the sail, through the upper hole in the mast, is used. The spare mast is shoved out and the luff of the jib made fast at its outboard end with the single sheet belayed where best positioned. The skipper, with his hand on the long tiller, sizes the main sheet and hauls in until the sail is 'filling and drawing'. He then holds it over his knee ready to ease or tighten as need be. Off she goes, the water fizzing as the many air bubbles burst alongside. You never hear that noise in a motor boat.

Now if you cast your mind back to where I was describing the beaching of a coble, I mentioned the thole pin on the port quarter, and said it had another purpose. Our coble is now under sail but the wind falls light and the crew is anxious to make as much head-way as they can. If the conditions are difficult i.e., tides and winds adverse, it may be required to fetch her on another tack with the wind on the opposite side. If so, the whole operation I have described is repeated but first with the sail being hauled down and shifted to the opposite side before it can be hoisted again. While the crew are busy doing this, the skipper has put the helm down to fetch her head over the wind. Not having enough headway, she doesn't make it, so the skipper ships an oar on the quarter thole pin, and with a few lusty strokes of the oar, he pushes her stern round so she is lying at the proper angle. Two tillers were carried, not as one writer said, as a spare, but because the long tiller was used when sailing, and the short one when working gear, so it did not get in the road.

The Yorkshire rig was different from ours although the boats were similar. As far as I know they used the two section oars, we called them the paddles, and their thole pins were higher. I never saw a metal thole pin on a coble until latter years when they were fitted with motors, and even then, only a few. They were of hardwood. My grandfather told me the best wood for wear was seasoned whitethorn or hawthorn. It had no grain, it polished well, and the fibres were well matted together. It makes splendid chisel handles, too. The Yorkshire rig did not use the double tack hook on the luff cringle. They had an arrangement where a rope passed through the holes in the big shoulder timbers across the boat from one side to the other. The tack cringle was fast in the centre of this rope, the ends taken to a gun tackle purchase on each side. By adjusting these purchases the tack could be shifted across from before the line of the mast to the weather gunnel, but no great tension could be given to the luff edge of the sail. Thus they had to use a gun tack purchase on the halliards, making four times the amount of rope to run before the sail was down. The sheet was the same arrangement, using the purchase, a double sheaver block at the clew cringle, and a single sheaved one at the inwaver.

The Northumbrian method was, in my mind, quicker and neater. I have seen a photograph in a magazine of a smallish coble being sailed in a moderate breeze showing the Yorkshire−style rig. I must confess it was something of a shock to see her with her sail abaft the mast, which was deliberate because the sheet was on the lee. A small jib, and the halliard going round the yards fore end to the masthead!. 'Good grief', I thought I had seen everything in my 80 years, but this!. The most dangerous situation one could ever be in in a sailing coble, bar losing the rudder. A sharp puff of wind and she would be capsized. It would have been no use letting go the sheet, there would still be too much sail on her, held by the mast. The old sailing men would turn in their graves. One lesson hammered home to us young ones was, never ever sail with the lug sail aft of the mast. Only the standing lug, with its tack to the foot of the mast, never the dipping lug. Needless to say, that boat was not 'sailing', she was just blowing along!. Where ignorance is bliss, 'tis folly not to take precautions........!

Well, that's the story of the Northumbrian coble and her rig, which I hope you have been able to follow. It was written by one of the last of them who started off in one rigged for sail. To explain every part would take another book. In my opinion our coble is the ultimate production of the Norse build. It was conceived by Norse minds, sailed by the descendants of those same Norsemen, our fore−fathers who came to this coast all those centuries ago.

One final word on the cobles before some bright spark gets on his hind legs and says, 'you're all wrong about the coble being unique to the north east corner of England, there is a similar type in Japan'. At the turn of the century, some Japanese business men on a fact finding tour of Britain, examined the cobles in Yorkshire. This was because a certain part of their coast was similar to ours and they made their version of the coble, using much the same principles for shallow beach landing. I have never seen either a photograph or a model of their effort but my uncle Jack Allen, my skipper and instructor in the old days, remembered their visit being reported in the newspapers of the day.

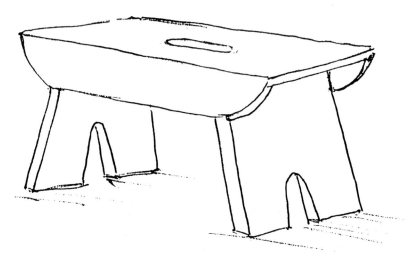

It was the custom in my father's day for a prospective bridegroom or newly married man to make a sturdy stool for the use of the household. It served a variety of uses, from a seat for the wife as she 'skeyenned' the bait, or for sitting bathing the children or any amount of other things. Usually they were about 2 feet long, 11 or 12 inches wide and about the same height. Our seat was made from part of a cabin locker seat from a wrecked sailing ship and is still in my possession.

I must mention, too, that we have a museum in Seahouses devoted to preserving a flavour of the old days. It is the brainchild of a local man, Selby Allan, from 'just ower the burn' at Beadnell. He has, virtually single-handed, made something of real value to the memory of the fishing. A museum is always a contrived assortment of artefacts all jammed up together but, Selby, in the limited space at his disposal, has somehow caught the atmosphere of the real